Capitalism and the Death Drive

Byung-Chul Han

Capitalism and the Death Drive

Translated by Daniel Steuer

polity

Originally published in German as *Kapitalismus und Todestrieb* © MSB Matthes & Seitz Berlin Verlagsgesellschaft mbH, Berlin 2019. All rights reserved.

This English edition © Polity Press, 2021

Excerpt from 'Tur mir Leid, aber das sind die Tatsachen' by Niels Boeing and Andreas Lebert in *Die Zeit* 5 (August 2014) © *Die Zeit*. Reprinted with permission of *Die Zeit*.

Interview 'Byung-Chul Han: COVID-19 has reduced us to a "society of survival"' by Carmen Sigüenza and Esther Rebollo, published on EURACTIV in May 2020 © EFE with EURACTIV. com. Reprinted with permission of EURACTIV.

Polity Press
65 Bridge Street
Cambridge CB2 1UR, UK

Polity Press
101 Station Landing
Suite 300
Medford, MA 02155, USA

ISBN-13: 978-1-5095-4501-8
ISBN-13: 978-1-5095-4500-1 (paperback)

A catalogue record for this book is available from the British Library.

Library of Congress Cataloging-in-Publication Data
Names: Han, Byung-Chul, author. | Steuer, Daniel, translator.
Title: Capitalism and the death drive / Byung-Chul Han ; translated by
   Daniel Steuer.
Other titles: Kapitalismus und Todestrie. English
Description: Cambridge, United Kingdom ; Medford, MA : Polity Press, [2021]
   | "Originally published in German as Kapitalismus und Todestrieb © MSB
   Matthes & Seitz Berlin Verlagsgesellschaft mbH, Berlin 2019"--Title page
   verso. | Includes bibliographical references. | Summary: "A leading
   cultural theorist examines the inherent destructiveness of capitalism"--
   Provided by publisher.
Identifiers: LCCN 2020053305 (print) | LCCN 2020053306 (ebook) | ISBN
   9781509545018 (hardback) | ISBN 9781509545001 (paperback) | ISBN
   9781509545025 (epub) | ISBN 9781509547661 (pdf)
Subjects: LCSH: Capitalism--Moral and ethical aspects. | Capitalism--Social
   aspects.
Classification: LCC HB501 .H33413 2021 (print) | LCC HB501 (ebook) | DDC
   330.12/2--dc23
LC record available at https://lccn.loc.gov/2020053305
LC ebook record available at https://lccn.loc.gov/2020053306

Typeset in 10.75 on 14 Janson Text by
Servis Filmsetting Ltd, Stockport, Cheshire
Printed and bound in Great Britain by Short Run Press

The publisher has used its best endeavours to ensure that the URLs for external websites referred to in this book are correct and active at the time of going to press. However, the publisher has no responsibility for the websites and can make no guarantee that a site will remain live or that the content is or will remain appropriate.

Every effort has been made to trace all copyright holders, but if any have been overlooked the publisher will be pleased to include any necessary credits in any subsequent reprint or edition.

For further information on Polity, visit our website: politybooks.com

CONTENTS

Conversations

ACKNOWLEDGEMENTS

'Capitalism and the Death Drive' appears for the first time in this volume.

'Why Revolution Is Impossible Today' was first published in *Süddeutsche Zeitung*, 3 September 2014.

'The Total Exploitation of the Human Being' was first published in *Süddeutsche Zeitung*, 20 June 2016.

'Inside the Digital Panopticon' was first published in *Der Spiegel* 02/2014.

'Only What Is Dead Is Transparent' was first published in *Die Zeit* 03/2012.

'Dataism and Nihilism' was first published in *Die Zeit* 40/ 2013.

'Torturous Emptiness' was first published in *Die Welt*, 30 December 2015, under the title: 'Quälende Leere: Narzissmus ist der Grund für Selfies und Terror' [Torturous Emptiness: Narcissism Is the Reason for Selfies and Terror].

'Jumping Humans' was first published in *Die Zeit* 04/2016.

'Where Do the Refugees Come From?' was first published in *Der Tagesspiegel*, 17 September 2015.

'Where the Wild Things Are' was first published in *Die Welt*, 8 September 2015.

'Who Is a Refugee?' was first published in *Frankfurter Allgemeine Zeitung*, 24 January 2017.

'Beauty Lies Yonder, in the Foreign' was first published in *Die Welt*, 24 November 2017, under the title 'Deutsche sollten Deutsche bleiben' [Germans Should Remain Germans].

'The Big Rush' was first published in *Die Zeit* 25/2013, under the title 'Alles eilt: Wie wir die Zeit erleben' [The Big Rush: How We Experience Time].

'In Your Face' was first published in *Blau: Ein Kunstmagazin* No. 9, March 2016, pp. 13–14.

'The End of Liberalism: The Coronavirus Pandemic and Its Consequences' appears for the first time in this volume.

'It Is Eros That Defeats Depression' was first published in *Philosophie Magazin* 05/2012 © Philosophie Magazin, Berlin 2012.

Capitalism and the Death Drive

What we nowadays call 'growth' is in reality random, cancerous proliferation. We are currently living through a frenzy of production and growth that seems like a frenzy of death. It is a simulation of vitality that conceals a deadly impending catastrophe. Production increasingly resembles destruction. Humankind's self-alienation may have reached a point 'where it can experience its own annihilation as a supreme aesthetic pleasure'.[1] What Benjamin said of fascism is today true of capitalism.

It is on account of our destructive rage that Arthur Schnitzler compares humankind to a bacterium. From this perspective, the history of humanity is like the progress of a deadly infectious disease. Growth and destruction become one and the same:

> Is it then not conceivable that, for some higher organism that we are incapable of grasping in its totality, and within which humankind finds the condition, necessity and meaning of its

1

own existence, humankind represents an illness that tries to destroy that organism and – the further it develops – must destroy it, the same way a bacterium seeks to annihilate the human individual who has been 'taken ill'?[2]

Humankind is blighted by a deadly blindness. We can only recognize the simpler levels of organization; regarding higher orders, we are as blind as bacteria. Thus, the history of humanity is an 'eternal battle against the divine', which is 'necessarily annihilated by the human'.

Freud would have shared every ounce of Schnitzler's pessimism. The human being, with his 'cruel aggressiveness', he writes in *Civilization and Its Discontents*, is a 'savage beast to whom consideration towards his own kind is something alien'.[3] Humankind annihilates itself. Freud may occasionally speak of the capacity of reason to recognize higher orders, but ultimately the human being is dominated by drives. For Freud, the death drive is responsible for our aggressive inclinations.[4] Only a few months after the completion of *Civilization and Its Discontents*, the Great Depression began. It would have provided Freud, one might think, with enough reasons to say that capitalism is that economic formation in which the savagery and aggression of the human being can best be expressed.

Given capitalism's destructiveness, it seems plausible to connect capitalism with Freud's death drive. In his study *Capitalisme et pulsion de mort* [Capitalism and death drive], the French economist Bernard Maris, who was killed in the terrorist attack on the offices of *Charlie Hebdo* in 2015, writes: 'The great cunning of capitalism . . . lies in the way it channels, it diverts, the forces of annihilation, the death drive, toward growth.'[5] According to Maris, capitalism uses the death drive for its own purposes, and this ultimately proves to be fateful. Over time, its destructive forces gain the upper hand and overwhelm life.

But is Freud's death drive really the right explanation for capitalism's destructive trajectory? Or is capitalism propelled by an altogether different kind of death drive, one that lies outside of Freud's theory of the drives? Freud's death drive has a purely biological basis. At some point in time – so he speculates – the properties of life were evoked in inanimate matter by a strong force acting on it. This introduced into the previously dead matter a tension that had to be resolved, and thus living beings came to possess a drive to return to the inanimate condition. The death drive was born: *"'The aim of all life is death"*, and, looking backwards . . . *"inanimate things existed before living ones".*[6] Against the backdrop of the death drive, all instances of life appear as mere 'myrmidons of death'. The drives of life have no aims of their own. Even the drives of self-preservation and mastery are partial drives whose function is 'to ensure that the organism shall follow its own path to death, and to ward off any possible ways of returning to inorganic existence other than those which are immanent in the organism itself'.[7] Every 'organism wishes to die only in its own fashion', and thus each organism resists any external influences that 'might help it to attain its life's aim rapidly – by a kind of short-circuit'.[8] Life is nothing but the organism's own being unto death. The idea of the death drive apparently held a lasting fascination for Freud. Despite some initial hesitation, he retained the idea:

> The assumption of the existence of an instinct of death or destruction has met with resistance even in analytic circles; . . . To begin with it was only tentatively that I put forward the views I have developed here, but in the course of time they have gained such a hold upon me that I can no longer think in any other way.[9]

3

The source of Freud's fascination was probably the fact that the idea of the death drive can help to explain human beings' destructive drive. Within the living being, the death drive works to bring about the being's dissolution. Freud interprets this processual death as an active self-destruction. Initially, then, the death drive expresses itself in the form of auto-aggression. It is only the drive towards life, Eros, that ensures that the death drive is directed towards external objects:

> In this way the instinct [i.e. the death drive – DS] itself could be pressed into the service of Eros, in that the organism was destroying some other thing, whether animate or inanimate, instead of destroying its own self. Conversely, any restriction of this aggressiveness directed outwards would be bound to increase the self-destruction, which is in any case proceeding.[10]

Freud makes no distinction between human beings and other living beings when it comes to the death drive: the drive inhabits *every* living thing, as that being's urge to return to the inanimate state. From the death drive, Freud deduces aggression, thereby making a connection between two very different impulses. An organism's inherent tendency to resolve a tension and, ultimately, to die does not necessarily suggest a destructive inclination. If we understand the death drive as a gradual reduction in vitality, then we cannot infer from it any destructive impulse. In addition, because the death drive is common to all living beings, it cannot explain what is specific about *human* aggression. Humans, however, are especially aggressive and, in particular, cruel. No other living being is capable of blind destructive rage. Freud also deduces sadism from the death drive:

4

It is in sadism, where the death instinct twists the erotic aim in its own sense and yet at the same time fully satisfies the erotic urge, that we succeed in obtaining the clearest insight into its nature and its relation to Eros. But even where it emerges without any sexual purpose, in the blindest fury of destructiveness, we cannot fail to recognize that the satisfaction of the instinct is accompanied by an extraordinarily high degree of narcissistic enjoyment, owing to its presenting the ego with a fulfilment of the latter's old wishes for omnipotence.[11]

The death drive inherent in every living being, the urge to return to the inanimate state, does not explain the decidedly narcissistic enjoyment that the ego takes in sadistic violence. In order to account for sadism, there must be an altogether different kind of destructive drive.

According to Maris, the driving force of capitalism is a death drive that serves the purposes of growth. But this does not tell us what brings about the irrational compulsion of growth itself: the compulsion that makes capitalism so destructive. What is it that forces capitalism blindly to pursue accumulation? At this point, death enters the frame. Capitalism rests on a negation of death. Capital is accumulated as a defence against death, against absolute loss. Death is what accounts for the compulsion of production and growth. Maris scarcely pays attention to death. Even Freud does not address death as such. The idea of the death drive, as a death wish, conceals the fear of death. Tellingly, Freud does not take into account the fact that every living being resists death. He remarks, somewhat oddly, that the idea of the death drive means '[w]e have no longer to reckon with the organism's puzzling determination (so hard to fit into any context) to maintain its own existence in the face of every obstacle'.[12] It is therefore not unreasonable to suggest that Freud's idea of a death drive ultimately represents an unconscious strategy for repressing the fact of death.[13]

The specifically human form of aggression, *violence*, is closely connected to the awareness of death, which is exclusively human. The economy of violence is ruled by a logic of accumulation. The more violence you exert, the more powerful you feel. Accumulated killing power [*Tötungsgewalt*] produces a feeling of growth, force, power [*Macht*] – of invulnerability and immortality. The narcissistic enjoyment human beings take in sadistic violence is based on just this increase in power. Killing protects against death. By killing, you arrest death. An increase in killing power means a reduction in death. The nuclear arms race also mirrors this capitalist economy of violence. Accumulating killing capacity is imagined as a way of accumulating a survival capacity.

The archaic economy of violence is exhibited in the spiralling violence of the blood feud. In archaic societies, every death is interpreted as the effect of a violent cause. Thus, even a 'natural' death may lead to revenge. The violence that led to the death is met with counter-violence. Every death weakens the group. Thus, the group must kill in turn in order to restore its feeling of power. Blood revenge is not an act of retribution, not a punishment. It is not a case of a perpetrator being held to account. Punishment is a rationalization of revenge; it stops revenge from escalating. Unlike punishment, blood revenge is undirected. That is the very reason it is so devastating. Sometimes, a group determined to avenge a death will kill individuals who were not involved in the death at all. Achilles took revenge for the death of his friend Patroclus by killing, and ordering killing, randomly. Not only enemies but also vast numbers of animals were slaughtered.

The etymology of 'money' points towards a connection with sacrifice and cultural rites. Money was originally the medium of exchange used for buying sacrificial animals.

Those with a lot of money acquired a divine power to kill: 'Looked at from the perspective of its roots in sacrificial cults, money is as it were frozen sacrificial blood. To throw money around, to let it flow and watch it flow, produces an effect similar to the flow of blood in fights or on sacrificial altars.'[14] The hoarded money gives its owner the status of a predator. It immunizes him against death. At the level of depth psychology, this archaic belief continues to operate in the idea that accumulated killing capacity, and accumulated capital assets, will ward off death. Capital's logic of accumulation corresponds exactly to the archaic economy of violence. Capital behaves like a modern version of mana. Mana is the name of that powerful, mysterious substance that one acquires through the act of killing. One accumulates it in order to create a feeling of power and invulnerability:

> The warrior was thought to embody the mana of all those whom he had killed . . . The mana of the warrior's spear was likewise increased with each death he inflicted. . . .; with a view to absorbing directly his mana, he ate some of his flesh; and to bind the presence of the empowering influence in battle . . . he wore as a part of his war dress some physical relic of his vanquished foe – a bone, a dried hand, sometimes a whole skull.[15]

The accumulation of capital produces the same affect as the accumulation of mana. Growing capital means growing power. More capital means less death. Capital is accumulated in order to escape death. Capital may also be seen as frozen time; infinite amounts of capital create the illusion of an infinite amount of time. Time is money: confronted with a time-limited life, we accumulate time-as-capital.

Adalbert von Chamisso's novella *Peter Schlemihls wundersame Geschichte* [*The Wonderful History of Peter Schlemihl*] can be read as an allegory of the capitalist economy. Schlemihl sells his shadow to the devil in return for a bottomless bag of gold (that is, infinite capital). The pact with the devil turns out to be a pact with capitalism. Infinite capital makes the shadow – which stands for the body and death – disappear. But Schlemihl soon realizes that a life without a shadow is impossible. He walks the earth as the undead. The moral is: death is a part of life. The story thus ends with this admonition: 'But you, my friend, if you want to live among mankind, learn to revere first your shadow, and then your money.'[16]

Capitalism is obsessed with death. The unconscious fear of death is what spurs it on. The threat of death is what stirs its compulsion of accumulation and growth. This compulsion drives us towards not only ecological but also mental catastrophe. The destructive compulsion to perform combines self-affirmation and self-destruction in one. We optimize ourselves to death. Relentless self-exploitation leads to mental collapse. Brutal competition ends in destruction. It produces an emotional coldness and indifference towards others as well as towards one's own self.

In capitalist societies, the dead and the dying are less and less visible. But death cannot simply be made to disappear. If, for instance, factories no longer exist, then work takes place everywhere. If mental asylums disappear, then madness has become normal. It is the same with death. If the dead are not visible, a rigor mortis has extended over all of life. Life freezes into survival: 'In survival, death is repressed; life itself ... would be nothing more than a survival determined by death.'[17]

The separation of life and death that is constitutive of the capitalist economy creates an *undead life, death-in-life*. Capitalism generates a paradoxical death drive; it deprives life of life.[18] A life without death, which is what capitalism strives to achieve, is what is truly deadly. Performance zombies, fitness zombies, and Botox zombies: these are manifestations of undead life. The undead lack any vitality. Only life that incorporates death is truly alive. The mania for health is the *biopolitical manifestation of capital itself.*

Capitalism's striving for life without death creates the *necropolis* – an antiseptic space of death, cleansed of human sounds and smells. Life processes are transformed into mechanical processes. The total adaptation of human life to mere functionality is already a culture of death. As a consequence of the performance principle, the human being ever more closely approximates a machine, and becomes alienated from itself. Dataism and artificial intelligence reify thinking. Thinking becomes calculating. Living memories are replaced with machine memories. Only the dead remember everything. Server farms are places of death. We bury ourselves alive in order to survive. In the hope of survival, we accumulate dead value, capital. The living world is being destroyed by dead capital. This is the death drive of capital. Capitalism is ruled by a *necrophilia* that turns living beings into lifeless things. A fateful dialectic of survival turns the living into the dead: the undead. Erich Fromm writes the following about a world ruled by necrophilia:

> The world becomes a sum of lifeless artifacts; from synthetic food to synthetic organs, the whole man becomes part of the total machinery that he controls and is simultaneously controlled by. . . . He aspires to make robots as one of the greatest achievements of his technical mind, and some specialists assure us that the robot will hardly be distinguished from living men. This achievement will not seem so astonishing when man himself is hardly distinguishable from a robot. The world of life has become a world of 'no-life'; persons have become 'nonpersons,' a world of death. Death is no

9

longer symbolically expressed by unpleasant-smelling feces or corpses. Its symbols are now clean, shining machines.[19]

Undead, death-free life is reified, mechanical life. *Thus, the goal of immortality can only be achieved at the expense of life.*

The capitalist system represses life, and it can only be ended by death. Baudrillard turns the death drive against Freud, radicalizing the concept such that it comes to denote a revolt against death: 'In a system that orders you to live and to capitalize life, the death drive is the only alternative.'[20] By risking death, the revolt of death cracks open the death-negating capitalist system and exposes it to the symbolic exchange with death. For Baudrillard, the *symbolic* is that sphere in which life and death are not yet divided from each other. The symbolic is opposed to the *imaginary* of deathless life. The revolt of death means that the capitalist system is shattered by the symbolic: 'Nothing, not even the system, can avoid the symbolic obligation, and it is in this trap that the only chance of a catastrophe for the system remains. . . . The system must *itself commit suicide in response to the multiplied challenge of death and suicide.*'[21]

The protagonists of Baudrillard's death revolt are suicidal characters of every kind. He even attributes a kind of subversive potential to terrorism. But a suicide bomber opposes the death-negating system with his *real* death. His violent end cannot open up the system to *symbolic* exchange with death. Terrorism is not a counter-image to the capitalist system; it is a phenomenon that is symptomatic of that system. The brutality and emotional coldness of the suicide bomber reflect the brutality and coldness of capitalist society. The attacker has the same psychogram as members of the general population. His suicide is a form of *self-production*, imagined as the ultimate selfie. The pulling of the trigger that detonates the bomb is akin to the push of the camera's button. The suicide

10

bomber knows that, immediately after the attack, his photo-graph will circulate in the media, and he will then receive the attention he had previously missed out on. A suicide bomber is a narcissist with an explosive belt. Thus, terrorism can be understood as the ultimate form of authenticity.

The revolt of death cannot unhinge the capitalist system. What is needed is another form of life, one that rescinds the division between life and death and reconnects the two. Every political revolution must be preceded by a revolution of con-sciousness, one that gives death back to life. The revolution must create an awareness of the fact that life is only truly alive when there is an exchange with death. It must demonstrate that the rejection of death destroys all living presence: 'The war against death takes the form of a preoccupation with the past and the future, and the present tense, the tense of life, is lost.'[22]

Death, understood as the biological end of life, is not the only, or only true, form of death. Death can also be under-stood as a continuous process in which one gradually loses oneself, one's identity, over the course of a lifetime. In this way, death may begin before death. The identity of a subject is a significantly more complex matter than is suggested by the stable name. A subject always keeps diverging from itself. The modern idea of death is based on biological functioning. Death is a matter of a body eventually ceasing to function.

Bataille understands death as an intense form of life. Death gives life intensity. It is an exuberance, excess, extravagance, indulgence, expenditure. Death provokes a rapture that is crucial in erotic experience: 'If love exists at all it is, like death, a swift movement of loss within us.'[23] Bataille opens his treatise *Eroticism* by stating: 'Eroticism, it may be said, is assenting to life up to the point of death.'[24] While Freud opposed Eros to the death drive, Bataille invokes the proxim-ity of death to Eros. If the impulse to live is intensified to the highest degree, it approaches the impulse to die, although, unlike Freud's death drive, Bataille views the latter impulse as itself an expression of life. The exchange between life and death takes place in the medium of eroticism. As exuberance and expenditure, death represents the principle of an anti-economy. Death has a subversive effect on the capitalist system: 'In a system where life is ruled by value and utility, death becomes a useless luxury, and the only alternative.'[25] Eroticism is an adventure of continuity. It breaks with the discontinuity of the isolated individual – the basis of the economy. Eroticism gives the self its death. Death is a *losing-oneself-in-the-other* that puts an end to narcissism.

The organization of capitalism depends on the desires and wishes that are reflected in consumption and production. Passion and intensity are replaced with comfortable feelings and consequence-free excitement. Everything is levelled out to fit the formula of consumption and enjoyment. Any negativity, such as pain, is removed in favour of the positivity of desire satisfaction. Death is the negativity par excellence. The compulsion of production abolishes negativity. Love is also accommodated to the capitalist process; it withers, becoming mere sexual desire. The other becomes just a sexual object for the narcissistic subject to use to satisfy its desire. Once the other is deprived of otherness, it can only be consumed.

By negating death, capitalism follows in the footsteps of metaphysics. Capitalism expresses a materialist metaphysics that strives for infinite capital. Plato already dreamt of a city without the dead. His ideal state rigorously discriminates against the dead. Any arable land, it says in *Laws*, should be free of graves. Graves have to be placed so as not to inconvenience the living. The dead may only be kept in the house for a maximum of three days, and only for as long as is necessary to rule out cases of suspended animation. Plato does not allow the living any symbolic exchange with death. Death is to be repressed, and the dead are a reminder of death. They are thus treated like waste that must be disposed of swiftly. But life that avoids death as if it were a pollution will suffocate in its own excrement.

Adorno opposes death-negating metaphysics with a form of thought that 'takes up in itself the undiminished, the non-sublimated awareness of death'.[26] Our repressed knowledge of death must be made conscious in all its severity. Human consciousness is mortal consciousness. Adorno knew that life that negates death as something purely destructive must itself develop destructive traits, that health is an ideology of capital – an illness, even. The hysteria of survival at all costs disfigures life. Adorno opposes the ugly cancerous growth of undead life with beauty that is innervated by the negativity of death:

> Exuberant health is always, as such, sickness also. Its antidote is a sickness aware of what it is, a curbing of life itself. Beauty is such a curative sickness. It arrests life, and therefore its decay. If, however, sickness is rejected for the sake of life, then hypostasized life, in its blind separation from its other moment, becomes the latter, destructiveness and evil, insolence and braggadocio. To hate destructiveness, one must hate life as well: only death is an image of undistorted life.[27]

Liveliness is friendliness. That life is friendly that is able to die.

Despite his ambivalent relationship with death, Freud is perfectly aware of the necessity of reconciling life with death. The unconscious repression of death must give way to the conscious acceptance of death:

> Would it not be better to give death the place in reality and in our thoughts which it is due, and to give a little

more prominence to the unconscious attitude towards death which we have hitherto so carefully suppressed? This hardly seems an advance to higher achievement, but rather in some respects a backward step – a regression; but it has the advantage of taking the truth more into account, and of making life more tolerable for us once again.[28]

To affirm life means also to affirm death. Life that negates death negates itself. Only a form of life that returns death to life will liberate us from the paradox of undead life: *we are too alive to die, and too dead to live.*

Why Revolution Is Impossible Today

At a recent debate between me and Antonio Negri at the Schaubühne in Berlin, two ways of critiquing capitalism clashed head-on. Negri was enthusiastic about the possibility of global resistance against the 'empire', the ruling neoliberal system. He presented himself as a communist revolutionary and called me a 'sceptical professor'. He emphatically invoked the 'multitude', the networked revolutionary masses and protest groups, apparently in the belief that this multitude could bring down the empire. To me, the revolutionary communist position seemed somewhat naïve and divorced from reality. I thus tried to explain to Negri why revolution is not possible today.

Why is the neoliberal system of rule so stable? Why is there so little resistance to it? Why does any resistance that emerges so quickly dissipate? Why, despite the growing gap between rich and poor, is revolution not possible? In order to explain this, we need a deeper understanding of how power and rule function today.

To establish a new system of rule, one must ensure there is no resistance. This is also true of the neoliberal system of rule. In order to inaugurate a new system of rule, what is needed is a positing power, and this often implies violence. But this positing power is not the same as the power that provides the system with its internal stability. It is well known that Margaret Thatcher, one of the pioneers of neoliberalism, regarded the trade unions as 'the enemy within' and fought violently against them. But this kind of violent assertion of the neoliberal agenda is not what constitutes neoliberalism's system-preserving power.

The system-preserving power of the disciplinary, industrial society was oppressive. Factory workers were brutally exploited by factory owners, and this violent exploitation prompted protest and resistance. In that situation, a revolution that would overturn the ruling relations of production was a possibility. In that system, it was clear who the oppressors, as well as the oppressed, were. There was a concrete opponent, a visible enemy who could serve as the target of resistance.

The neoliberal system of rule is structured in an altogether different fashion. The system-preserving power is no longer oppressive but seductive. It is no longer as clearly visible as it had been under the disciplinary regime. There is no longer a concrete opponent, no one who is taking away the freedom of the people, no oppressor to be resisted.

Out of the oppressed worker, neoliberalism creates the free entrepreneur, the entrepreneur of the self. Today, everyone is a self-exploiting worker in his own enterprise. Everyone is both master and slave. The class struggle has been transformed into an internal struggle against oneself. Those who fail blame themselves and feel ashamed. People see themselves, rather than society, as the problem.

Disciplinary power, attempting to control people by force,

by subjecting them to a dense matrix of orders and prohibitions, is inefficient. Much more efficient is that technique of power that ensures that people subordinate themselves to the system of rule voluntarily. The exceptional efficiency of this technique derives from the fact that it does not work through prohibition and deprivation but through pleasure and fulfilment. Instead of making people docile, it tries to make them dependent. This neoliberal logic of efficiency also applies to surveillance. In the 1980s, people still protested en masse against the census. Even schoolchildren took to the streets.

From today's perspective, the information requested by the census – profession, qualifications, how far one lives from one's workplace – seem almost risibly innocuous. There was a time when people felt themselves to be confronting a state, a ruling institution, that was trying to wrest information from its citizens. That time has long since passed. Today, we expose ourselves voluntarily. It is precisely this felt freedom that makes protest impossible. Unlike those protesting against the census in the eighties, we do not significantly resist surveillance. Voluntary self-disclosure and self-exposure follow the same principle of efficiency as voluntary self-exploitation. Against what should we protest? Against ourselves? The American conceptual artist Jenny Holzer expresses this paradoxical situation in one of her 'truisms' thus: 'Protect me from what I want.'

It is important to make a distinction between positing and preserving power. System-preserving power has now taken on a smart, friendly form, and it has thereby become invisible and unassailable. The subordinated subject is not even aware of its subordination. It believes itself to be free. This technology of rule is a highly efficient way of neutralizing resistance. Forms of rule that oppress people and undermine freedom are unstable. What makes the neoliberal regime so stable, so impervious to resistance, is that it makes use of freedom instead of suppressing it. Restricting freedom quickly provokes resistance. Exploiting freedom does not.

Following the financial crisis in Asia, South Korea was paralysed and in shock. Then the IMF came along and provided a bailout. In return, the government had to implement neoliberal reforms, and to use force against the resulting protests. This kind of oppressive power is positing power, and it often involves the use of force. But this positing power differs from system-preserving power, which, in the case of the neoliberal regime, presents itself as a form of freedom. According to Naomi Klein, the state of shock that societies like South Korea and Greece find themselves in after catastrophes such as the financial crisis are the perfect opportunity to forcibly subject these countries to radical reprogramming. In South Korea, there is no longer any real resistance to these measures. Instead, one finds high levels of conformism and consensus – together with depression and burnout. South Korea currently has the highest suicide rate in the world. Instead of seeking to change society, people use violence against themselves. The outward aggression that might have provided a basis for revolution has instead given way to auto-aggression.

There is no cooperative, networked multitude that could serve as a global protest movement and revolutionary body. Rather, the current form of production is based on the solitary, isolated, disconnected entrepreneur of the self. It used to be the case that, although enterprises competed with each other, there was solidarity within each enterprise. Today, everyone is in competition with everyone else, even within a single enterprise. This universal competition may lead to an enormous increase in productivity, but it destroys solidarity and the sense of community. You cannot form a revolutionary mass out of depressive, disconnected individuals.

Neoliberalism cannot be explained in Marxist terms. It

does not even exhibit the famous 'alienation' from work. We throw ourselves enthusiastically into our work until we burn out. The enthusiasm is, in fact, the first stage of burnout. Burnout and revolution are mutually exclusive. It is therefore wrong to believe that the multitude will throw off the parasitic empire and establish a communist society.

What is the state of play regarding communism today? Everywhere there is talk of 'sharing' and 'community'. The sharing economy is supposed to be replacing the economy of property and ownership. 'Sharing is caring': this is one of the maxims of the 'circlers' in Dave Eggers's novel *The Circle*. The cobblestones on the way to the headquarters of the Circle company are interspersed with tiles bearing slogans such as 'Find Community' and 'Participate'. But really the slogan should be 'Caring is Killing'. The digital ride-sharing platform WunderCar, which seeks to turn every one of us into a taxi driver, makes use of the idea of 'community' in its advertising. But the advent of the sharing economy does not herald the end of capitalism or the creation of a more communal global society in which sharing is valued above ownership, as Jeremy Rifkin claims in his book *The Zero Marginal Cost Society*.[1] On the contrary, the sharing economy ultimately leads to the commercialization of all aspects of life.

The transition from ownership to 'access', which Rifkin celebrates, does not liberate us from capitalism. Whoever lacks money also lacks access to sharing. Even in the age of access, we are still living within the 'ban-opticon'; those without money are still excluded.[2] Airbnb, the community marketplace that encourages people to turn their homes into hotels, even economizes human hospitality. The ideology of community, or of a collaborative commons, leads to the total commodification of community. Simple, purposeless friendliness becomes impossible. In a society in which everyone rates everyone else, friendliness is commercialized. People become friendlier in order to receive better ratings. Even at the very heart of the collaborative economy, the relentless logic of capitalism still rules. Paradoxically, despite all this wonderful 'sharing', no one gives anything away. Once it begins to sell communism itself as a commodity, capitalism has reached its culmination. Communism as a commodity: that spells the end of any revolution.

The Total Exploitation of the Human Being

'Customer lifetime value' is the term used to describe the value a human being represents for a company over the course of a lifetime. Underlying this concept is the intention of transforming the whole of the human being's life into commercial value. Today's hypercapitalism transforms all of human existence into a network of commercial relations. There is no area of life that can escape commercialization.

The increasing digitization of society makes the commercial exploitation of human life easier, expanding and accelerating the process. It subjects areas of life that were previously inaccessible to economic exploitation. What is necessary today, therefore, is the creation of new areas of life, even new forms of life, that resist the total commercial exploitation of human life.

Apple's flagship store in New York is in every respect a temple to hypercapitalism. It is a cube made entirely of glass. Inside, it is empty. It thus represents nothing but its own transparency. The actual shop is located in the basement. The building is the principle of transparency made material.

The translucent Apple store is perhaps the architectural counter-image of the Ka'bah in Mecca, with its black curtain, the Kiswah. Ka'bah literally means 'cube'. The black building is not at all transparent. The cube is also empty. It represents a theological order that stands in opposition to the hypercapitalist order.

The Apple store and the Ka'bah represent two different forms of rule. The transparent cube is meant to represent freedom. It symbolizes limitless communication. But this transparency is itself a form of rule, one that, today, takes the form of a digital totalitarianism. The transparent cube announces a new rule: the rule of hypercapitalism. It symbolizes today's total communication, which is gradually coming to mean total surveillance and total exploitation.

The Ka'bah is closed. Only priests have access to the inside of the building. The transparent cube, by contrast, is open 24/7. Anyone may enter it as a customer. Here we have two different ruling orders: rule by closure and rule by opening. The latter is more efficient than the former, however, because it pretends to offer freedom. The glass cube is hypercapitalism's celebration of a hypercommunication that pervades, exposes and monetizes everything. Here, with the transparent cube atop the shop in the basement, communication, commercialism and consumption coincide.

Global companies collect data on consumer behaviour, marital status, profession, preferences, hobbies, living conditions and income. The algorithms they use do not differ significantly from those of the US National Security Agency.

The world-as-department-store turns out to be a digital panopticon that subjects us to total surveillance. Total exploitation and total surveillance are two sides of the same coin. The marketing company Acxiom divides people into seventy economic categories. The group of people with the lowest value as customers are called 'waste'.

Big Data makes it possible to predict human behaviour. The future can thus be calculated and manipulated. Big Data turns out to be a highly efficient psychopolitical instrument that allows one to manipulate other human beings like marionettes. Big Data produces a sort of knowledge that facilitates mastery over others, making it possible to intervene in and influence the human psyche without the person noticing. Digital psychopolitics degrades the human person into an object that is quantifiable and controllable. Big Data thus heralds the end of the free will.

Sovereign is he, the jurist of constitutional law Carl Schmitt wrote, who decides on the exception.[1] Much later, he revised his famous statement: 'After the Second World War, and facing my death, I now say: "Sovereign is he who decides on the [distribution of] waves in space."'[2] Carl Schmitt apparently spent his life afraid of the manipulative effects of radio and television. Today, in the age of the digital regime, the statement on sovereignty would have to be revised yet again: sovereign is he who decides on the flow of data in the network.

Digital interconnectedness allows for every aspect of a person to be rated and exposed. This sort of personalized data collection presents considerable risk, and so it must be strictly regulated. The activities of credit scoring companies such as Schufa also have a discriminatory effect.[3] The economic evaluation of a person contradicts the idea of human dignity. No one should be degraded into an object of algorithmic evaluation.

The ulterior motives that drive Schufa, an institution whose quasi-holy status is taken for granted in Germany, may be inferred from the fact that, some time ago, the company had the idea that it could garner useful information by trawling through people's social media posts. Their advertising slogan – 'We create trust' – is pure cynicism.

Companies like Schufa destroy all trust and replace it with control. To trust someone means that I maintain a positive relationship with him despite my relative ignorance about him. Trust enables me to act in the absence of knowledge. If I already know everything about a person, trust is redundant. Schufa processes more than 200,000 queries every day. That is only possible in a control society. A society based on trust would not need companies such as Schufa.

To trust someone implies the possibility that one's trust will turn out to have been unfounded, that is, the possibility of betrayal. But the possibility of betrayal is constitutive of trust itself. Freedom also implies a certain risk. A society that submits everything to control and surveillance in the name of security becomes totalitarian.

In the face of the growing threat of digital totalitarianism, the President of the European Parliament, Martin Schulz, recently urged states to formulate a charter of fundamental rights for the digital age.[4] The former minister of the interior Gerhard Baum also demanded a comprehensive reduction in data collection and processing – a data disarmament.

What are needed now are new and radical approaches to avoiding data totalitarianism. Technological fixes to ensure that personal data is automatically deleted after a certain amount of time should also be sought. This would lead to a thoroughgoing data disarmament, something we sorely need in these times of data frenzy.

By itself, a charter of fundamental digital rights will not be enough to prevent data totalitarianism. We must also bring about a change in consciousness and mindset. We are not simply inmates or victims of a digital panopticon that is controlled from elsewhere.

The original panopticon was Jeremy Bentham's design for

a type of prison. The prisoners are housed in an outer ring and observed from a central tower inside the ring. In the digital version of the panopticon, we are not simply imprisoned. Rather, we are active participants. We take part in building the digital panopticon. By exposing ourselves, by hooking ourselves up and voluntarily uploading our body-related data to the net, like the millions of devotees of the 'quantified self' movement, we actually maintain the digital panopticon. This new form of rule does not force us to be silent. Rather, it constantly asks us to communicate, to participate, to express our opinions, desires, wishes and preferences – even to narrate our lives.

In the 1980s, everyone in Germany was up in arms about the census. An office was even bombed. Even pupils took to the streets. There were mass demonstrations.

From today's vantage point, this reaction seems incomprehensible. The information requested was innocuous – one's profession, qualifications, marital status and the distance between one's home and workplace. Today, we do not object when hundreds of thousands of sets of data related to us are collected, stored, passed on and sold. No one is up in arms about it. There are no mass protests against Google or Facebook.

During the census protests, people felt that the state, the ruling institution, was attempting to scrutinize them against their will. Those days are long gone. Today, we voluntarily expose ourselves, without the need for any pressure or official decree. We put all sorts of data and information about ourselves online voluntarily, without knowing who knows what, and when, about us.

The lack of control over our data represents a serious crisis for freedom. Such is the quantity of the data we now produce that the concept of data protection has become obsolete. We are now not just the victims of state surveillance but active elements of the system. We voluntarily surrender protected private spaces and expose ourselves to pervasive digital networks that scrutinize us.

As a new form of production, digital communication seeks to dismantle protected spaces and transform everything into information and data. Through this process, all protective distance is lost. In the context of digital hypercommunication, everything is mixed up with everything else. The borders between inside and outside become more and more permeable. Humans become interfaces within a totally interconnected world. Hypercapitalism furthers and exploits this digital defencelessness.

We must ask ourselves, very seriously, what kind of life we want to live. Do we want to continue to give ourselves up to total surveillance and total exploitation, and thus forfeit our freedom and our dignity? It is time to organize a collective resistance to the looming digital totalitarianism. Georg Büchner's words are as relevant as they ever were: 'We are puppets, our strings are pulled by unknown forces; we ourselves are nothing, nothing!'[5]

Inside the Digital Panopticon

Today, everything is 'smart'. Soon we shall live in smart cities, where everything – yes, everything, without exception – will be interconnected: not only humans but also things. We will receive emails not only from friends but also from household appliances, domestic animals and the food in our fridge. All this will be made possible by the internet of things. In the smart city, we will all walk around with Google glasses. Everywhere and at every moment we will be provided with useful information, without having to ask for it. We will be guided to the restaurant, to the bar, to the concert hall. The data glasses will also take decisions for us. In combination with a dating app, they will even bring us more success and efficiency in matters of love and sex.

Data glasses will scan our visual field for useful information. We will all become happy hunters of information, and in the process we will adopt the perspective of the hunter. Areas of our visual field that are not likely to contain information will be ignored. Contemplative lingering, dwelling on things, which is a recipe for happiness, will be completely replaced by the hunt for information. Human perception will finally achieve total efficiency, no longer distracted by objects that deserve little attention and presumably hold little information. The human eye itself will become an efficient search engine.

The internet of things represents the completion of the transparency society. The transparency society has become indistinguishable from a society of total surveillance. Everything around us observes and surveys us, tracking what we do and do not do. The fridge, for instance, will know our eating habits, the networked toothbrush the details of our dental hygiene regime. These things will actively record all aspects of our lives. In the digital control society, data glasses will be surveillance cameras and smartphones will be bugs.

Today, every click of the mouse is recorded. Every step we take can be reconstructed. We leave digital traces everywhere. Our digital habitus is completely captured online. The total recording of life will replace all trust with information and control.

Trust makes it possible to entertain relations with other people in the absence of complete knowledge about them. Because digital networks make it so easy to obtain information, trust becomes less and less important as a social practice. It gives way to control. There is therefore a structural affinity between the transparency society and the control society. Where information is easy to obtain, the social system is transformed from one based on trust to one based on control and transparency.

The place of Big Brother is taken by Big Data. The constant and comprehensive recording of life fully realizes the transparency society. It resembles a digital panopticon.

The idea of the panopticon dates back to the British philosopher Jeremy Bentham, who, in the eighteenth century, designed a prison that facilitated the total surveillance of all the inmates. The prison cells are arranged in a circle around a watchtower, which provides total vision to the warden – a kind of big brother *avant la lettre*. In order to discipline the inmates, they are isolated from each other and are not allowed to speak with each other. The inhabitants of the digital panopticon, by contrast, communicate ceaselessly and expose themselves voluntarily. The digital control society makes great use of freedom. This sort of society is only possible thanks to voluntary self-disclosure and self-exposure.

In the digital control society, pornographic self-presentation and panoptic control coincide. The control society is fully achieved when its inhabitants communicate not because of compulsion from outside but because of an inner need – that is, where the fear of having to forsake one's private and intimate sphere gives way to the need shamelessly to expose it, where freedom and control become indistinguishable.

The warden of Bentham's panopticon can only observe the inmates physically. He does not know what goes on inside them. He cannot read their minds. In the digital panopticon, by contrast, it is possible to access the thoughts of the inhabitants. That is what makes the digital panopticon so efficient, and it is what makes possible the psychopolitical control of society.

Today, the demand for more transparency is issued in the name of freedom of information or democracy. In truth, transparency is an ideology; it is a neoliberal dispositif. It violently drags everything out into the open in order to transform it into information. In the context of today's immaterial mode of production, more information and communication mean greater productivity, acceleration and growth.

Secretiveness, strangeness or alterity represent obstacles to limitless communication. They are thus removed in the name of transparency. The dispositif of transparency exerts a compulsive force that tends to bring about conformity. It is part of the logic of transparency that it brings about a large degree of consensus. Total conformity is the result.

'Newspeak' is the name of the ideal language in George Orwell's surveillance state. Newspeak must totally replace 'oldspeak'. The purpose of newspeak is to limit the horizon of thought. Offensive thoughts are to be made impossible by removing the words necessary for their formulation. Thus, for instance, the word 'freedom' is removed. This already makes clear the difference between Orwell's surveillance state and today's digital panopticon: the latter makes liberal use of 'freedom'.

Orwell's surveillance state, with its telescreens and torture chambers, is something altogether distinct from the digital panopticon, with its internet, smartphones and Google glasses. The digital panopticon is dominated by a semblance of limitless freedom and communication. Here, there is no torture – only posting and tweeting. A surveillance that coincides with freedom is much more efficient than Orwellian surveillance, which is directed against freedom.

The neoliberal regime's technology of power is not prohibitive or repressive but seductive. It uses smart power. It seduces rather than prohibits. It affirms itself not by making people obey it but by making people like it. By consuming and communicating, even by clicking a 'like' button, we submit ourselves to this form of rule. Smart power closely follows the contours of the psyche; it flatters the psyche instead of repressing or disciplining it. It does not force us to be silent. Instead, it constantly prompts us to communicate, share, participate – to express our opinions, desires and wishes and to narrate our lives. We are confronted with a technology of power that does not negate or suppress our freedom but that exploits our freedom. This is what has created the current crisis of freedom.

Orwell's surveillance state is dominated by the principle of negativity. Ours is dominated by the principle of positivity: desire is not repressed but excited; communication is not repressed but maximized. Instead of confessions gained through torture, we have the voluntary exhibition of the private sphere and the digital exposure of the soul. The torture chamber is replaced by the smartphone.

Bentham's Big Brother is invisible to the inmates, but in their minds he is omnipresent. In the digital panopticon, by contrast, no one really feels as though they are under surveillance. It is therefore not quite right to characterize today's digital panopticon as a 'surveillance state'. In the digital panopticon, we feel free. But this feeling of freedom, wholly absent from Orwell's surveillance state, is a problem. It stops resistance from forming.

In 1987, there were fierce protests against the census in Germany. Today, surveillance parades as freedom, and freedom turns out to be control.

The Apple commercial broadcast during the Super Bowl in 1984 has acquired near-mythic status. The ad presents the company as liberating us from Orwell's surveillance state. Apathetic, submissive workers march in lockstep into a large hall, where they watch a fanatical speech by Big Brother on a telescreen. Suddenly, a female runner holding a sledgehammer, and being pursued by the thought police, storms into the hall. Unperturbed, she runs on, carrying the sledgehammer in front of her heaving chest. Resolute, she approaches Big Brother, before spinning around several times, hammer throw-style, and releasing the sledgehammer, sending it flying into the screen, which explodes into a wall of white light. The people in the hall are stirred from their lifelessness, and a voice announces: 'On January 24th, Apple Computer will introduce Macintosh. And you'll see why 1984 won't be like "1984".'[1] But 1984 did not mark the end of the surveillance state. It heralded the beginning of a new kind of control society, one far more efficient than Orwell's surveillance state.

It was recently revealed that the NSA referred to Steve Jobs as 'Big Brother' in their internal communications. The documents also referred to mobile phone users as 'zombies', and spoke, quite logically, of 'smart phone exploitation'.

But the NSA is not the real problem. It is not just Google and Facebook but also Big Data companies like the global marketing firm Acxiom that are frenetically collecting our data. In the US alone, Acxiom holds data on 300 million citizens – in other words on almost everyone in the country. 'Create a 360-degree view of your customers', as one of the company's panoptic commercial slogans has it.[2] In the face of these developments, Edward Snowden is neither a hero nor a criminal. He is a tragic phantom in a world that has become a digital panopticon.

Only What Is Dead Is Transparent

It is hard to think of a more ubiquitous catchword in contemporary public discourse than that of 'transparency'. It is mentioned and emphasized, in particular, in connection with the freedom of information. But to reduce transparency to questions of corruption and democracy is to miss its true importance. Transparency manifests itself as a systematic compulsion that takes hold of all social, economic and political processes and subjects them to far-reaching transformation.

The transparency society is a society of positivity. Things become transparent when they shed all negativity, when they are smoothed and levelled out, when they allow themselves to be enveloped by smooth flows of capital, communication and information without offering any resistance. Actions become transparent when they subordinate themselves to a calculable and controllable process. Things become transparent when they shed their singularity and find expression solely in their price. Images become transparent when they are deprived of any hermeneutic depth, even of meaning, and thus become pornographic. The positivity of the transparency society makes it a hell of the same.

Communication reaches its maximum velocity where the same answers the same, where there is a chain reaction of the same. The negativity of what is different or alien, the resistance of the other, interferes with and delays the smooth communication of the same. Transparency stabilizes and accelerates the system by eliminating what is other, what deviates. An entry in Ulrich Schacht's diary reads: 'A new word for Gleichschaltung [coordination]: transparency.'[1]

The word transparency derives from the Latin words *trans* and *parere*. *Parere* originally means: to appear or be visible in response to someone's order. Someone who 'pariert' is visible and obeys without offering any resistance.[2] At its etymological roots, there is something violent about the word transparency. Today, transparency is, accordingly, an instrument of control and surveillance.

Strangely enough, the unfortunate television interview that Christian Wulff, the president of the Federal Republic, gave to journalists from ZDF and ARD resembled a police interrogation.[3] Wulff repeatedly emphasized that 'he wanted to create trust through transparency'. The motto of the public campaign for a transparency law is: 'Transparency creates trust.' This motto contains a contradiction. Trust is only possible in a state that lies somewhere between knowing and not knowing. If I know everything up front, trust is redundant. Transparency is a state in which all not-knowing is eliminated. Where transparency reigns, there is no space for trust. The slogan should thus run: 'Transparency destroys trust.'

The more trust disappears, the more vociferous the calls for transparency become. The transparency society is a society of distrust that, as trust diminishes, must rely increasingly on control. For a political figure who enjoys the deep trust of the population, a call for even the most modest level of trans-

34

parency would be demeaning. Louder calls for transparency point to the fact that society's moral foundation has become brittle and that moral values like honesty and candour are becoming less and less important. In place of the authority that morality once held, we have transparency as the new social imperative.

The call for transparency is accompanied by pressures of acceleration. The conventional political parties and their ideologies and power structures are too slow and inflexible. The so-called liquid democracy of the Pirate Party can be seen as an attempt to counteract the sluggishness and rigidity of party politics. The Pirate Party's website illustrates the practice of liquid democracy very well:

> In questions concerning tax law, I would like to be represented by the SPD, for environmental policies by the Green Party, and regarding educational policies by a private person, Mr Müller. Regarding the decision on the new law governing university admissions I would like to cast the vote myself.[4]

In truth, liquid democracy, without assemblies or powerful decision-makers, would signal the abolition of the principle of party-based representative democracy. Expert knowledge would replace political will formation. Political parties would be no more important than the private person, Mr Müller. They would no longer be political parties.

We can also put it like this: the Pirate Party is an anti-party. It is the first party without its own colour. Transparency is colourless. In the Pirate Party, colours that stand for ideologies are prohibited; only colours that stand for ideology-free opinions are permitted. The acceleration and increased flexibility promised by liquid democracy implies the possibility of quickly changing one's colours depending on the situation.

Liquid democracy makes decision-making faster and more flexible, but ultimately it degenerates into the democracy of 'like' clicks.

In the course of implementing liquid democracy politics gives way to an administration of social needs that leaves the existing socio-economic structures untouched and instead persists within them. Transparency is a very effective stabilization mechanism. Simply increasing access to information does not bring about systemic renewal or change. Transparency lacks the negativity necessary to call the existing political and economic system into question.

The post-privacy ideology that demands the complete abandonment of the private sphere in the name of transparency is no less naïve. It would be worthwhile reminding the representatives of this new online movement that human beings are not even transparent to themselves. According to Freud, the ego negates what the unconscious categorically affirms and desires. The 'id' remains mostly hidden from the ego. Thus, there is a rift within the human psyche; the psychic system is never at one with itself. This fundamental rift, the source of opacity, makes the self-transparency of the ego impossible. The self-transparency of the ego is an illusion, albeit perhaps a necessary illusion. There is also a yawning rift between people. It is therefore impossible – and it would not be desirable – to create interpersonal transparency.

It is the opacity of the other that keeps a relationship alive. Georg Simmel writes:

> The mere fact of absolute knowledge, of having psychologically exhausted everything, sobers us up, even without prior intoxication; it paralyzes the vitality of relations. . . . The fertile depth of relationships senses and honors something even more ultimate behind every ultimate revelation . . . But this depth is only the reward for that tenderness and

self-discipline that still respects the inner private life of the other, even in the most intimate relationship that involves the whole person, and that allows the right to ask questions to be limited by the right to secrecy.[5]

Given that an ethic of transparency has taken hold of contemporary society, an ethic of distancing is required.

It seems that the human soul needs to have spheres in which it can be alone with itself without having to care about the gaze of the other. Total exposure makes the soul wither. Total transparency may well lead to a kind of burnout of the soul. This is the meaning behind Peter Handke's remark: 'I live off what the others don't know about me.'[6] Only machines are fully transparent. But the human soul is not a machine. Inwardness, spontaneity and eventfulness, the very constituents of life, are opposed to transparency. Human freedom, in particular, makes total transparency impossible. Apart from that, a transparent relationship would be a dead relationship, without any attraction. Only what is dead is transparent. The acknowledgement that there are positive, productive spheres of human being and being-with that are utterly destroyed by the compulsion of transparency would be a moment of enlightenment.

Strictly speaking, the only fully transparent thing is emptiness. In order to avoid this emptiness, large amounts of information are put into circulation. The more information is released, the more blurred and chaotic the world becomes. The mass of information does not illuminate the darkness. Transparency is not a light but an invisible radiation that pervades everything, rendering it see-through instead of illuminating it. Transparency [Durchsichtigkeit] does not bring about clear-sightedness [Hellsichtigkeit].

Julian Assange, in a conversation with the philosopher Peter Singer published in *Philosophie Magazin*, makes a surprising confession: that he is 'not actually a big fan of transparency'. Rather, his beliefs are based on the 'meagre philosophy' that 'history shows that when human beings pass on information that is true about their environment to each other they are providing themselves with the means to make good decisions about the environment in which they live'. Assange is apparently sceptical towards the kind of transparency that has today become totalizing and ideological. He also notes that the internet has become a sophisticated mass surveillance system that spreads like a 'cancerous growth'.[7]

For the avoidance of misunderstanding: there is nothing objectionable about transparency in the name of fighting corruption or defending human rights. In those contexts, it is to be welcomed. The critique of transparency aims at transparency as ideology – fetishized, total transparency. The fact that the transparency society threatens to turn into a control society is a particular cause for concern. Surveillance cameras turn us all into suspects. The naked body revealed by the airport security scanner is a symbol of our times. The internet turns out to be a digital panopticon.

Everyone must reveal themselves – that is the logic of the control society. The control society reaches its culmination when subjects expose themselves not because they are compelled to do so from without but because of a desire generated from within: that is, when the fear of losing one's intimate private sphere gives way to the desire shamelessly to expose oneself. The control society obeys the logic of efficiency that rules performance-oriented societies. Self-exploitation is more efficient than exploitation by others because it is accompanied by a feeling of freedom. The performance-oriented subject is compelled from within, voluntarily. This dialectic of freedom is also the foundation of the control society. Self-exposure is more efficient than being exposed by others because it is accompanied by a feeling of freedom.

The compulsion of transparency is ultimately not an ethical or political imperative but an economic one. Exposure is exploitation. The one who is fully exposed is subjected to limitless exploitation. The over-exposure of people maximizes economic efficiency. The transparent customer is the latest inmate, the *homo sacer* of the economic panopticon. The panopticon of the transparency society differs from that of the disciplinary society in that it does not require any shackles, walls or locked rooms. Unlike the isolated inmates of Bentham's panopticon, the inhabitants of the transparency society are constantly connected with each other. It is not loneliness but hypercommunication that guarantees transparency.

The peculiarity of the digital panopticon consists in the fact that its inhabitants actively take part in building and maintaining it by exhibiting and exposing themselves. Surveillance therefore does not come in the form of an attack on freedom, as Juli Zeh and Ilja Trojanow suggest.[8] Rather, freedom and control coincide – just as the transparent user is at once perpetrator and victim. Everyone joins in to build the panopticon of the digital network.

Dataism and Nihilism

Today's frenzied data collection activities are not limited to the NSA. They are an expression of a new faith, which one might call dataism, that is becoming almost a religion, almost totalitarian. The euphoria over the possibilities of Big Data also expresses this faith of the digital age.

Data is collected for every conceivable purpose. The NSA, Acxiom, Google and Facebook of course have an uncontrollable hunger for data, but the followers of the 'quantified self' movement, for instance, have also succumbed to dataism. They equip their bodies with sensors that automatically record body temperature, steps, sleeping patterns, calorie intake, movement profile and even brain waves: everything is measured. Even while a person meditates, the heart rate is recorded. Thus, even during relaxation, performance and efficiency are what counts – a paradox, actually.

Sensors not only cover our bodies. More and more of them can be found in our environment. They transform us into data. At the same time, we hover in a strange realm of meaninglessness, and we throw ourselves into hyperactivity and hypercommunication.

Can all this data actually enable us to better understand ourselves? Even in antiquity, it was thought that keeping records about oneself was an essential part of caring for oneself. The Roman author Tertullian called this *publicatio sui*: the exploration of the self and the unsparing publication of all thoughts. The sinner was meant to present himself as a sinner, and thus liberate himself from his sin.

Christian self-disclosure goes hand in hand with a renunciation of one's self-serving ego in favour of a higher plane of meaning. *Ego non sum, ego*: I am no longer me. By renouncing the lower ego, one reveals a higher ego. *Publicatio sui* was a practice of truth. The self-disclosure of antiquity was committed to a higher plane of meaning, just as the asceticism of antiquity was not a mere diet.

The quantified self movement, by contrast, is simply about optimizing physical and mental performance. Even with the benefit of all this data, the self-optimizers fail to truly care for themselves. The recording techniques of the quantified self are those of a self that has become self-referential.

The ego, in itself, cannot yield any meaning. The collected data does not answer the question 'who am I?' Using a smartphone as a mobile confessional neither provides any self-knowledge nor any access to truth.

Data on its own, no matter how comprehensive it may be, does not yield knowledge. It cannot answer those questions that go beyond matters of performance and efficiency. In this sense, data is blind. Data alone yields neither meaning nor truth. Nor does it make the world more transparent. Quite the contrary, the world today seems more opaque than ever. We find it increasingly difficult to distinguish between what is important and what is not. We are at the mercy of almost completely automatic processes. We optimize ourselves without really knowing what purpose this optimization serves.

The knowledge provided by data is a limited, rudimentary form of knowledge. It is not even enough to allow us to discern causal connections. Big Data seems to promise absolute knowledge; in reality, it produces absolute ignorance. It is impossible to orientate ourselves using Big Data.

We communicate intensively, almost compulsively. Lapses in communication seem unbearable to us. They reveal an emptiness that must be bridged with more communication and more information.

Dataism probably goes hand in hand with a form of nihilism. Dataism is the result of a renunciation of meaning and context; data is meant to fill the vacuum of meaning. The entire world disintegrates into data, and we gradually lose sight of any broader contexts. In this sense, dataism and nihilism are two sides of the same coin.

Torturous Emptiness

Self-harm, in the form of cutting, has become a widespread phenomenon among today's youth. Millions of young people in Germany injure themselves. Inflicting wounds on oneself provides a deep sense of relief. The usual method is to cut one's arm with a razor blade. Cutting is becoming a real form of addiction.

As with all addictions, the tendency is for the interval between hits to become shorter and shorter, and for the dose to increase. The cuts become deeper and deeper. The afflicted feel a 'pressure to cut'. How can such self-harm be reconciled with the narcissism that increasingly characterizes the contemporary individual?

The self-harmers often suffer from depression and anxiety disorders. They are tortured by feelings of guilt, shame and low self-esteem. As a result of a persistent sense of inner emptiness, eventually they do not feel anything at all. Only when they cut do they feel something again.

People suffering from depression or borderline personality

disorder (BPD) often complain that they 'do not feel themselves'. Among those who self-harm, large numbers of people
have depression or BPD. Cutting clearly seems to be a desperate attempt to feel oneself again, to restore a feeling of
self. The body sheds red tears. I bleed therefore I am.

What is the origin of this torturous feeling of emptiness?
First, it is important to distinguish between narcissism and
self-love. The subject of self-love distances itself from others.
It maintains clear borders that distinguish between 'me' and
'not me'. In the case of a narcissistic self-relation, by contrast,
others are distorted until the self can recognize itself in them.
The narcissistic subject perceives the world as something
that, in various ways, resembles itself.

The fateful consequence of this is that the other disappears.
The border between self and other becomes blurred. The self
becomes diffuse and vague. A stable self only emerges in
confrontation with others. An excessive, narcissistic relation
to self, by contrast, produces a feeling of emptiness. The ego
drowns in the self.

Today, libidinal energy is predominantly invested in the
ego. The narcissistic accumulation of ego libido leads to a
decrease in object libido, that is, libido that cathexes, that is
invested in objects. Object libido creates an object attachment that, in turn, stabilizes the ego. Without any object
attachment, the ego is left to its own devices, a situation that
creates negative feelings such as anxiety or emptiness.

There are many social forces that lead to the pathological narcissistic accumulation of ego libido we see today:
for instance the imperative of authenticity, which creates a
narcissistic compulsion to focus on the self, to constantly self-
question, to listen to oneself, to lay siege to oneself, and – not
least – to accuse oneself.

Ultimately, authenticity is a neoliberal strategy of production. The ego is permanently forced *to produce itself* as an

entrepreneur of the self. Whoever fails in this picks up the razor blade.

Many adolescents are plagued by vague fears: the fear of failure, of being left behind, of making mistakes or of having made the wrong decision, of not living up to their own expectations. They are ashamed of their inadequacies. Cutting is also a ritual of self-punishment.

The lack of self-esteem that is at the root of self-harm suggests a general gratification crisis in our society.[1] Every one of us needs to be loved. One's ego is only stabilized when one is loved by others. The narcissistic, self-referential focus on the ego, by contrast, destabilizes it.

In order to enjoy a stable sense of self-esteem, I have to take myself to be important. But this means I also have to think that others take me to be important. This may be a rather vague idea, but it is indispensable to the feeling that one *is* important. The absence of this feeling of being [Seinsgefühl] is what is responsible for self-harm. Cutting may simply be a cry for love.

Self-esteem is not something that I can produce on my own. I have to rely on being rewarded by others who love me, praise me, acknowledge me and appreciate me. Narcissistic isolation, the instrumentalization of others and rampant competition between individuals make impossible a climate in which people can be appropriately rewarded.

The performance-oriented subject is compelled to achieve ever more. It thus never reaches a satisfying point of completion. The subject lives with a permanent lack, and with feelings of guilt. Because it is competing not only against others but – primarily – against itself, it tries to get ahead of itself.

Primary gratification, which resists all quantification, is today also more and more difficult to obtain. It comes about through, for instance, true friendship. Friendship is a relationship with an other that stabilizes and fulfils the ego. The 'friends' one has on social media lack the negativity of the other. They form an applauding mass. Their otherness is erased in the 'like'.

The feeling of emptiness leads to depression. The depressive performance-oriented subject feels its self to be a heavy burden. A narcissistic congestion of ego libido makes it ill. It is tired of itself, exhausted by itself. Completely incapable of taking a position outside of itself, it becomes tangled up in itself. This leads, paradoxically, to a hollowing out of the self.

Enclosed in itself, caught up in itself, the subject loses all relation to others. I touch myself, but I only feel myself through the touch of another person. The other is essential to the formation of a stable self. If the other disappears, the ego ends up in emptiness.

Some people only feel their own bodies when they cut themselves. Our relationship towards our own bodies, it seems, has been disrupted. The body is completely subject to the logic of optimization. We thus become alienated from our bodies. The body is utilized instead of inhabited. Bulimia and anorexia are pathological signs of this development. Cutting is a desperate attempt at feeling one's own body again.

Today, every form of harm is avoided. This also applies to love. To fall in love – that would already be to risk too much harm. We keep the stakes low because we fear loss and the pain and hurt it would cause us.

Communication is smoothed out into courteous remarks, into positivities. Negative feelings, such as grief, do not find expression, are not voiced.

But love without harm is inconceivable. Love attacks and wounds. Today, the other, as a source of harm, is avoided. But the harm we seek to avoid returns, and it returns in the form of self-harm, which, unlike harm caused by others, can at least be inflicted in a controlled way.

Contemporary society is characterized by the attempt to abolish all negativity. Everything is smoothed out. The smooth lacks the negativity of opposition. It ceases to be something standing against us [Gegen-Stand].[2] The French '*objection*', like the English 'objection', expresses a protest, whereas everything smooth aims to please. The smooth is not an object. If negative feelings such as grief cannot be expressed or voiced, cutting frees those feelings from their muteness.

According to Alain Ehrenburg, the prevalence of depression is due to the absence of conflict. Today's culture of performance and optimization does not allow for any engagement with conflict because this culture already makes too many demands on our time. The performance-oriented subject knows only two states: functioning well and failing. In this respect, it resembles a machine. Machines do not experience conflict either: they run smoothly or they are broken.

Conflicts, however, produce relationships and identities. A person grows and matures by dealing with conflict. What is seductive about cutting is that it releases accumulated destructive tensions quickly, without the need for time-intensive work to deal with conflict. Chemical processes in the brain, the secretion of endogenous drug-like substances, are said to be responsible for this rapid release of tension.

But tensions soon return, and thus so too does the compulsion to cut. Cutting functions in a similar way to antidepressants, which also suppress conflictual conditions and quickly allow the depressive performance-oriented subject to function again.

If we turn to selfie addiction, we find that it also has little to do with self-love. It is simply an expression of an idling, narcissistic ego that can never come to rest. Inner emptiness leads to a vain attempt to *produce oneself*. This attempt at self-production must fail; the only thing that is reproduced is the emptiness itself. Selfies are manifestations of the self as an empty form. They intensify the feeling of emptiness.

Selfie addiction has its roots not in self-love but in narcissistic self-reference. A selfie is the beautiful, smooth surface of an emptied, wholly insecure self. Today, in order to escape torturous emptiness, one reaches either for the razor blade or for the smartphone. Selfies are smooth surfaces that, at least for a moment, present the empty self in a favourable light. But when we turn them over we find them covered in bleeding wounds. Thus, wounds are the reverse side of selfies.

Could it be possible that the suicide attacks in Paris were a perverse attempt at feeling oneself again, at restoring a self-esteem that had been destroyed, at bombing or shooting the heavy burden of emptiness out of existence? Is it possible to compare the psychology of terror with that of the selfie and self-harm, both of which are also directed against the empty self? Do the adolescents who self-harm, that is, turn their aggression against themselves, have the same psychogram as the terrorists?

As we know, boys, unlike girls, tend to turn their aggression outwards, against others. Suicide attacks are, then, paradoxical acts in which auto-aggression and aggression against others, self-production and self-destruction, become one: an extreme form of aggression that is nevertheless imagined to be, at the same time, the ultimate selfie.

Detonating the bomb is like pushing the button that takes the selfie. At that moment, the imaginary world is in charge, for the real world, with all its discrimination and hopelessness, is no longer worth living in.

Jumping Humans

These days people being photographed, especially young people, seem to jump around wildly. A Google search for 'people jumping' yields innumerable astonishing photographs of humans leaping around in all possible variations. The phenomenon of jumping in photos seems to have spread like an epidemic.

Why do people today jump up in front of cameras? Are we not afflicted with fatigue and depression? Are they really jumping for joy? Is jumping an expression of the increasing vitality of our society? Or are these jumps rather pathological twitches of the narcissistic ego?

In earlier times, when photos served primarily as mementos, people being photographed presented themselves in a calm and civilized manner. No one would have dreamt of jumping around. The aim of a photograph was mainly to preserve the moment in order to be able to remember it later. People held back, and the event came to the fore. They receded behind the moment or occasion that was to be remembered. No one wanted to present themselves, let alone make an exhibition of themselves. No one was vying for attention. Those photos were of cult value, not exhibition value.

In his famous essay on 'The Work of Art in the Age of Its Technological Reproducibility', Walter Benjamin points out that *'in photography, exhibition value begins to drive back cult value on all fronts'*, although

> cult value does not give way without resistance. It falls back to a last entrenchment: the human countenance. It is no accident that the portrait is central to early photography. In the cult of remembrance of dead or absent loved ones, the cult value of the image finds its last refuge. In the fleeting expression of a human face, the aura beckons from early photographs for the last time. This is what gives them their melancholy and incomparable beauty. But as the human being withdraws from the photographic image, exhibition value for the first time shows its superiority to cult value.[1]

For those things that are in the service of a cult it is more important that they are present than that they are exhibited and seen. Their cult value depends on their existence and not on the fact that they are exhibited. In our society, however, in which things, having all become commodities, must be exhibited in order even to *be*, exhibition value becomes an absolute value. Everything that rests in itself, stays within itself, ceases to have value. Things only acquire a value if they are exhibited and seen. Human beings also behave like commodities; they exhibit themselves, produce themselves,[2] in order to increase their exhibition value.

The human countenance and its cult value have now completely disappeared from photography. The age of Facebook has turned the human countenance [Antlitz] into a *face* that is nothing more than its exhibition value.[3] The *face* is the exhibited human face [Gesicht] without the aura of its gaze, the commodity form of the human countenance [Antlitz]. Intrinsic to a gaze is an inwardness, a reserve, a distancing. Thus, a gaze cannot be exhibited. If the human face [Gesicht] is to be commodified into a *face*, the gaze must be destroyed.

The phenomenon of people jumping in photographs can be explained in terms of the contemporary frenzy of exhibition. The moment or the event that was the object of the cult of remembrance is disappearing. Everyone jostles for attention and exhibits themselves. After all, each of us is supposed to be a brand. As a result, photography becomes worldless. The world becomes merely a pleasant backdrop for the ego.

We are witnessing the development of a kind of photography that is free of remembrance and history, a photography that is permanently on the hop, so to speak, that has an altogether different temporality, which lacks width and depth, a photography that exhausts itself in moments of fleeting emotion, a photography that is not narrative but only deictic. In jumping up, the whole body serves as it were as an index finger that points to itself.

For Roland Barthes, the essence of photography is that it says: 'this is how it was'. That is what gives it its cult value. The digital image, by contrast, has no age, no fate and no death. It is characterized by a permanent presence and present. It is no longer a medium of remembrance but a medium of exhibition, like a shop window.

In a fragment titled *Homesickness without a home – the wanderer*, Nietzsche writes: 'This God they once created for themselves out of nothing – no wonder! – He has become a nothing to them. Overhasty, like jumping spider monkeys.'[4] These spider monkeys Nietzsche also called the 'last men'. They resemble 'cattle': 'they leap about . . . fettered to the moment and its pleasure or displeasure'.[5] Today, Nietzsche's

51

'last men' leap about in front of the camera. A new human being is emerging: *homo saliens* – jumping man. From his name we would suppose he was a relative of *homo sapiens*, but he is devoid of the virtues of understanding and wisdom that characterized *homo sapiens*. He jumps for attention.

Where Do the Refugees Come From?

After the financial crisis of 2008 hit, spectacular measures were rapidly implemented to bail out the banks that were at risk. The EU countries provided 1.6 trillion euros to save the banks from bankruptcy – equivalent to 13 per cent of the EU's GDP. The financial crisis cost Germany alone 187 billion euros.

When the survival of the banks was at stake, Europe was determined and prepared to make sacrifices. When human lives are at risk, however, Europe acts less decisively. Angela Merkel's clear commitment to provide aid for refugees, which she made last Tuesday, was the exception to the rule. But in light of the refugee crisis it is important to bear in mind the extent to which the West is responsible for the misery from which people are fleeing.

Consider Africa, the continent from which the majority of boat refugees are coming. The European colonialism that caused such unspeakable suffering in Africa continues, in effect, to the present day, if in a more subtle and globalized form. Once, the European colonial powers divided up the African continent by drawing arbitrary borders, and thus creating conflict. Even after the end of colonial rule, Europeans and the US continued to support despots for decades in order to protect their interests. Nowadays, political instability in Africa is due to the greed for cheap natural resources, which is to blame, in part, for the continent's extraordinarily deadly wars. States like the two Congos have disintegrated into territories controlled by warlords who enlist child soldiers. Those warlords strike business deals with Western entrepreneurs seeking raw materials, for whom ethnic conflicts are merely a side issue.

The rare-earth metals used in our much-loved smartphones, tablets and gaming consoles are mined under wretched working conditions. In this exploitative production, which takes place mainly in China, all industrial countries nevertheless have a hand. The wealth of the West rests on the misery of others, an asymmetry that is constitutive of global capitalism. Violence and injustice are immanent to the system. An equitable distribution of global wealth would contradict the logic of capital.

In 2013, France sent troops to Mali. On the face of it, their aim was to fight against Islamist terrorism. But in this case, too, mineral resources played a significant role. In neighbouring Niger, the state-owned French corporation Areva produces uranium that fuels Europe's nuclear energy industry. The spoil from the uranium mining is simply left lying around in the open. Clouds of contaminated dust hover over the land. As early as 2010, *Der Spiegel* reported that the 'Areva clinic' was keeping quiet about the cancer risk associated with uranium mining and was registering cancer deaths as caused by malaria. In his *Betting on Famine: Why the World Still Goes Hungry*, Jean Ziegler explains in impressive detail how it is that famines are still able to occur all over the world.[1] They often result from the policies of the IMF, which aim to open up markets in the Global South to multinational food corporations. But this free trade ruins local economies, leading to hunger and death. Seen from this angle, the 2015 Milan Expo, which aimed to fight world hunger with new technology, is pure cynicism.[2]

Or let us take the example of Eastern Europe: in 1999, NATO bombed Kosovo without a UN mandate, with the Bundeswehr taking part in the raids. The comprehensive reconstruction of the country promised by the German government, however, never materialized. Now Germany sends back Kosovan refugees fleeing their homeland.

Or let us look at the Middle East: in 2011, Europe's military intervention in Libya plunged the country into chaos. The present chaos in Iraq was preceded by the Iraq War, a war that had been justified by the West on the basis of blatant lies. Iraq was an ethnically and religiously unstable country with a high potential for conflict, a product of British colonial rule – like Afghanistan in the nineteenth century. In the case of Afghanistan, it was the subsequent Russian intervention in the twentieth century that turned a civil war into a proxy war between the Soviet Union and the US-backed mujahideen.

Now, people are fleeing the Taliban. But, again, in this case the West is not altogether innocent. In their study *Living Under Drones*, legal scholars from Stanford University and New York University conclude that pre-emptive strikes by drones do not reduce the terrorist threat – and in fact even increase it, because they fuel resentment and hatred.[3] As more civilians are killed, the ranks of the terrorists swell. All the while, civilians' everyday lives are ruled by fear.

At present, 'Islamic State' is without a doubt the greatest threat, and this threat too was made possible by the Iraq War. We should also remember that radical Islam and neoliberal capitalism are two sides of the same coin. Al-Qaeda's motto – 'We love death as you love life' – draws attention to the fact that radical Islamism and consumer society, with its mania for health, which turns living into a meaningless bare life that must be prolonged at any cost, are mutually dependent. Money alone does not provide one with an identity. Those who are left behind are not only without identity but also without hope. Tellingly, a group of young people from Dinslaken, where there are high levels of youth unemployment, went to fight in the 'holy war'.

Finally, let us turn to Syria, where the civil war has developed into a proxy war involving Russia, Iran, the US and the Gulf states. In this context, one must bear in mind that the oil-rich Gulf states are also outposts of global capitalism, where millions of immigrants from Asia and Africa toil like slaves in order to create wealth for their host states.

Celebrating our welcoming culture, applauding our empathy or accusing certain EU countries of a lack of solidarity – none of this solves the real problem. Emotions are short-sighted and short-lived. Only reason is far-sighted, and what we need is a politics dictated by reason. The endless debate over quotas is a sideshow masking an absence of policy. And erecting border fences replaces politics with policing and declares refugees to be criminals. Only decisive action, guided by reason, can put an end to the proxy war in Syria and the unspeakable misery of the refugees. Europe should show more self-confidence in this area and, given its history, must shoulder more of the global responsibility for dealing with the issue – or risk a rude awakening.

Where the Wild Things Are

In light of increasing conflict around the world and the intensifying refugee crisis, Kant's famous essay 'Perpetual Peace' is extraordinarily and especially relevant today. His plea on behalf of reason has lost nothing of its significance. Enlightenment, guided by reason, is still a work in progress.

Confronted with conflicts around the world, many people are painfully aware that humanity has still not achieved the right use of reason, that it has not yet even alighted on reason. For Kant, reason is what ends the state of war, the state of nature, and 'sets up peace as an immediate duty'.[1] The league of nations proposed by Kant is a 'pacific federation (*foedus pacificum*)' guided by reason. It differs from a 'peace treaty (*pactum pacis*)' in that it ends not only one war but the state of war, that is, the state of nature:

> Peoples who have grouped themselves into nation states may be judged in the same way as individual men living in a state of nature, independent of external laws; for they are

a standing offence to one another by the very fact that they are neighbours. Each nation, for the sake of its own security, can and ought to demand of the others that they should enter along with it into a constitution, similar to the civil one, within which the rights of each could be secured. This would mean establishing a *federation of peoples*.[2]

For Kant, attempts to justify war, even if hypocritical, are already proof 'that man possesses a greater moral capacity, still dormant at present, to overcome eventually the evil principle within him' because 'otherwise the word *right* would never be used by states which intend to make war on one another'.[3]

Kant also believed that peace would be promoted by the *'spirit of commerce'*, which 'cannot exist side by side with war' and 'sooner or later takes hold of every people'. Because war is detrimental to trade, *'financial power'* compels the state to prevent it. The peace thereby achieved, however, does not derive from 'motives of morality' but from 'mutual self-interest'. It is not a case of reason but of 'nature' guaranteeing 'perpetual peace by the actual mechanism of human inclinations'.[4] Reason, by contrast, does not enjoin us to act in accordance with self-interest, and that is why it stands in opposition to subjective 'inclinations'.

For Kant, the European Union – a free trade zone and community based on a treaty between governments that advances the individual interests of the constituent nation states – would not count as an entity based on reason. It would only count as a reason-based organization if it were transformed from a treaty-based community into a community based on a democratic constitution in which humanist values, such as human dignity and equality, were enshrined: that is, a moral constitution. The 'financial power' and 'commercial spirit' that prevail in the EU today, however, hinder such a development. The EU will only be transformed into a reason-based and constitution-based community if it rejects the power of money, the hegemony of capital.

Kant's idea of perpetual peace culminates in his demand for universal 'hospitality': that every foreigner should have a *'right of resort'* in any country. A person may stay in a foreign country and 'must not be treated with hostility, so long as he behaves in a peaceable manner'. According to Kant, 'no one originally has any greater right than anyone else to occupy any particular portion of the earth'.[5] The globalization of the earth, which Kant actually predicted, has to proceed in tandem with the development of a cosmopolitan constitution.

Kant points out, in particular, 'the *inhospitable* conduct of the civilised states of our continent, especially the commercial states': 'the injustice which they display in *visiting* foreign countries and peoples (which in their case is the same as *conquering* them) seems appallingly great'.[6] In this passage, Kant excoriates the European states for their cruel and exploitative actions and for the inhumane practice of slavery, saying they 'drink injustice as if it were water' and at the same time 'wish to be considered *as* chosen believers'.[7] They did not behave like guests in foreign countries; they behaved like robbers. Unlike these 'European savages', as Kant calls them, the refugees or asylum seekers that come to Europe today behave like guests and are peaceful.[8] That, at least, would be Kant's judgement.

Hospitality is not some utopian idea, and it does not rest on philanthropy. It is an idea enjoined on us by reason itself: 'As in the foregoing articles, we are here concerned not with philanthropy, but with *right*. In this context, *hospitality* means the right of a stranger not to be treated with hostility when he arrives on someone else's territory.'[9] The idea of hospitality is not fantastic and overstrained; it is a necessary complement to the unwritten code of political and international right, transforming it into a universal right of humanity. Only under this condition can we flatter ourselves that we are continually advancing towards a perpetual peace.[10]

The inhospitable conduct of many European states in the current refugee crisis represents a grave danger, a menacing regression – something approaching a new form of barbarism.

Reason in the Kantian sense prescribes general rules that allow those following them to transcend their self-interest. The EU's refugee policies risk failure because some member states cling to their self-interest instead of following reason. Self-interest is not a category of reason but of the understanding. The pursuit of self-interest may be rational, but it is not reasonable. It is not moral. Those who are guided by their self-interest are not acting according to 'motives of morality'.[11] Self-interest is a human 'inclination' that must be overcome in favour of reason. Following our inclinations makes us unfree. Only in virtue of self-legislating moral reason can we be free. In the face of the current refugee crisis, it has recently been said: 'Those who only feel empathy lack understanding.'[12] Kant would respond: 'Those who only have understanding lack reason.' And if someone drew attention to the significant costs of taking in an unaccompanied refugee child, then Kant would respond by drawing attention to the child's dignity, which must be respected at any cost. Cost is a category of the understanding; dignity is a category of reason.[13]

Trade associations point out that Germany would profit from immigration, that refugees would increase the supply of skilled workers and that immigration may even lead to the demographic rejuvenation of rural areas. Refugees would bring more advantages than disadvantages. This may well be the case, but any discussion about the right way to deal with refugees must be conducted independently of such cost-benefit analysis.

To talk in terms of 'benefits' is to reduce decisions taken on the basis of reason to mere calculation. Moral reason should take precedence over the calculating understanding. Morality differs fundamentally from business and calculation. In a certain sense, morality is blind; therein lies its incorruptible power, its humanity.

In contemporary hypercapitalism all that matters is price. Dignity has no place. Capital rules over everything. Businesses use the term 'lifetime value' to refer to the overall value to be gained from customers if every aspect of their lives is commercialized. The human person is reduced to customer value, or market value. The term expresses the aim of translating the whole person, the entirety of a life, into mere commercial value. Hypercapitalism dissolves all of human existence into a network of commercial relations. There is no area of life today that has escaped commercial exploitation. Hypercapitalism turns all human relations into commercial relations. It deprives human beings of dignity, replacing it with market value. The world has become one gigantic department store. Would the EU, the European department store, open its doors to refugees? Refugees probably have no rightful place in a department store.

Germany will only be able to continue to consider itself a civilized, reason-based nation if it strictly adheres to its moral values, such as the ideal of human dignity. It is demanded of us not just to demonstrate solidarity or empathy but, in the first instance, to follow the dictates of reason. Reason is far more stable and reliable than mere empathy. The refugee crisis could even be a significant historical opportunity for Germany to demonstrate to the world that it is a reliable, morally mature country in which reason reigns.

The populist response to the refugee crisis is a betrayal of reason. Politicians like Viktor Orbán eschew reason altogether, regressing to the stage of Kant's 'European savages'. And in those right-wing extremists who attack refugees and engage in wanton violence Kant would probably see a case of 'barbarism, coarseness and brutish debasement of humanity' resurfacing.[14]

In an appendix to 'Perpetual Peace' that has hitherto generated little comment – 'On the Disagreement between Morals and Politics in Relation to Perpetual Peace' – Kant draws attention to the need to unite politics and morality. For Kant, morality is the 'epitome of absolutely binding laws',[15] and politics cannot 'take a single step without first paying tribute to morality'.[16] Today, morality and politics come apart, because politics does not submit itself to the laws of reason but only to economic compulsion. The economy is not a category of reason. In the economic sphere, morality gives way to a 'general doctrine of expediency', a 'theory of the maxims by which one might select the most useful means of furthering one's own advantage'. And this amounts to a denial 'that morality exists'.[17]

Politics is withering away. In the terminology of Luhmann's systems theory, it has become a subsystem, whose medium is power, while the economy has become a supersystem that swallows up all subsystems. Even the system of morality seems to have been incorporated into that supersystem – after all, morality sells. As a subservient subsystem, politics has little ability to influence the economic system. It is totally dependent on it. What little room for manoeuvre there is within the political subsystem is used simply to retain power. All means at politicians' disposal are used to hold on to power. In this context, having a vision may even be a hindrance.

Politics must submit itself again to the 'motives of morality' and the corresponding values of solidarity, justice and human dignity. This would require it to resist 'financial power', the hegemony of capital, or at least to make sure capital takes a back seat. A politics devoid of morality reduces the EU to a market, a department store, and allows injustice to grow. But a department store [Warenhaus] is not a guest house [Gasthaus]. Europe must rise above the 'commercial spirit', above self-interest, and prove itself to be a guest house.

Who Is a Refugee?

'We Refugees' is the title of an essay by Hannah Arendt first published in 1943 in *The Menorah Journal*. This essay was Arendt's compelling farewell to the traditional notion of the refugee. She writes:

> A refugee used to be a person driven to seek refuge because of some act committed or some political opinion held. Well, it is true we have had to seek refuge; but we committed no acts and most of us never dreamt of having any radical political opinion. With us the meaning of the term 'refugee' has changed. Now 'refugees' are those of us who have been so unfortunate as to arrive in a new country without means and have to be helped by refugee committees.[1]

She and her fellow 'refugees' preferred to be called 'newcomers' or 'immigrants'. What Arendt has in mind here is an altogether new idea of the refugee, one that we perhaps have still not arrived at yet. It is simply someone who goes to a new country in the expectation of a better life.

Arendt describes the figure of the 'optimistic' refugee as follows:

> The more optimistic among us would even add that their whole former life had been passed in a kind of unconscious exile and only their new country now taught them what a home really looks like. . . . With the language, however, we find no difficulties: after a single year optimists are convinced they speak English as well as their mother tongue; and after two years they swear solemnly that they speak English better than any other language – their German is a language they hardly remember.[2]

Seeking to forget their past, these refugees avoid 'any allusion to concentration or internment camps', lest this be interpreted as an indication of 'pessimism'.[3] Arendt quotes a compatriot who had founded one of the so-called 'societies of adjustment' as saying: 'We have been good Germans in Germany and therefore we shall be good Frenchmen in France.'[4] The ideal immigrant, according to Arendt, is like that 'woman of tidy size [who] is delighted with every new dress which promises to give her the desired waistline'.[5]

I was myself an optimistic refugee in Hannah Arendt's sense. In my new country I sought a life that was not available to me in my country of birth where the structures of social expectations and conventions would not have permitted me to live, or even to think, in a wholly or radically different way. I was twenty-two at the time. After studying metallurgy in Korea, I wanted to study philosophy, literature and theology in Germany. While on the campus of my university in Seoul, I would often look up to the sky and think that it was too beautiful for me to spend my whole life under it as a metallurgist. I was dreaming of a more beautiful life, a better life. I wanted to think about life philosophically. I took flight to Germany. I arrived without means and without the language – I spoke hardly any German back then – at the age of twenty-two.

Like all optimistic refugees, I was at first socially isolated. Social isolation hurts. I thus feel I understand the pain of today's refugees. I empathize with them. With my poor German, it was difficult to find my way into the structures of society. In settling in Germany, which was something I wanted to achieve (I would rather not speak about so-called 'integration'), a lack of linguistic competence was the main obstacle I faced. I then came to believe that love would prove the best settling strategy. If I could find a German woman who loved me, I naïvely thought, she would listen to me and could quickly teach me the German language, for she would want to understand what I thought about her, what I felt about her, etc. I was almost greedy for every new German word: my ambition was to speak just like a German. As is well known, Willy Brandt also employed this strategy. Within only a few months of his exile, he was writing articles and speeches in Norwegian. While living underground in Berlin, under the pseudonym Gunnar Gaasland, he spoke German with a Norwegian accent. It was clearly not only just his linguistic talent but also his linguistic hunger, and his hunger for love, that, in his case, did so much to speed up the process of language acquisition.

A year after my arrival in Germany, I was sure, like Hannah Arendt's optimistic refugee, that I spoke German better than any other language. Patriotism is another thing that, for Arendt, is purely 'a matter of routine or practice'. Her 'ideal immigrant' is the one who 'always, and in every country into which a terrible fate has driven him, promptly sees and loves the native mountains'.[6] He is a patriot, a lover of the land. He loves the country in which he establishes himself. I, too, love this land. One day, I applied for my naturalization, giving up my Korean passport in the process. Now, I am German. Now, I speak German better than my mother tongue, which is now truly my pure 'mother language': it is only with my mother that I still speak Korean. My mother tongue has become alien to me. I love Germany. I would even call myself a patriot, a lover of the land. At any rate, I am more patriotic than Petry, Gauland and Höcke combined.[7] Their populism degrades Germany, my country, a country that, in my experience, has always been very hospitable.

People who were good citizens in their country of origin will also be good citizens in their new country. We should continue to welcome these 'newcomers'. People who were already criminals in their country of origin, like Anis Amri, will continue to be criminals in their new country.[8] We shall turn them away. For the newcomers, however, we should provide an environment in which they can become good citizens.

But what does it mean to be a good citizen? I am the second Korean professor at the Berlin University of the Arts. The first was Isang Yun, an important composer. He was also politically active. In the 1960s, he was protesting against the military dictators who then ruled South Korea. In 1967, he was kidnapped, in the middle of Germany, by the South Korean secret service. In Seoul, he was sentenced to life in prison. After his early release, he returned to Germany, having been stripped of his South Korean citizenship by the regime. He became a refugee, and he obtained German citizenship. Maybe, like Hannah Arendt, he would have denied that he was a refugee. 'I am a good, optimistic immigrant', he might have said, like Hannah Arendt. His German was impeccable.

What makes a good citizen is a good ethos. A good citizen possesses moral values such as a love of freedom, fraternity and justice. Even if the actions of the good citizen are criminalized by the ruling political system, he remains a good citizen in virtue of his moral (in the Kantian sense) ethos, and he remains a patriot, someone who loves the land and the people.

During the last years of his life, Isang Yun despaired about the eruption of xenophobia in post-unification Germany. He was dismayed by the crowds applauding outside the hostel for Vietnamese contract workers in Rostock-Lichtenhagen that had been set alight. He was disappointed, because he loved Germany. To me, too, the events in Rostock resembled a pogrom. At present, I watch with concern as xenophobia flares up again, in response to the large numbers of incoming refugees in Germany and in other European countries. What I would like to do best is to find another dream land, to flee to a hospitable country where I can be a wholehearted patriot again, a lover of the land.

Beauty Lies Yonder, in the Foreign[1]

What is Europe? How can Europe be defined? All liberal parties today are committed to Europe. But what is this thing to which they are committed? A geographically defined continent? Or an idea?

If Europe rests on an idea, which idea is it? Where does Europe begin, and where does it end? Russia, for instance, despite the continent's current concerted attempts to distance itself economically and militarily from the country, is geographically as well as culturally part of Europe.

Is there really no alternative to Europe? The alternative to Europe, just like the alternative for Germany, is today firmly claimed and practically monopolized by right-wing populist parties.[2]

Is there really no alternative to Europe that could be supported wholeheartedly by liberal parties? In contemporary political debates, Europe wanders around like a phantom, an idea devoid of conceptual clarity.

Is it possible to be more precise, if not in geographical

terms then at least in conceptual ones, about what Europe means? When we take a closer look, however, Europe is a spectre.

To begin with, the name 'Europe' points us back to the Greek *europe*, a composite noun made up of *eurys* (wide) and *ops* (view). Europe thus essentially means 'the one with the broad view'.

A beautiful name, really. According to Greek mythology, Europe is the name of a Phoenician princess who was kidnapped and taken to Crete in the shape of a Taurus. Europe's distant ancestor, paradoxically, came from the Orient.

As a geographical term, 'Europe' initially denoted only the Peloponnese, before the Greek geographer Herodotus extended it to cover the continental landmass north of the Mediterranean Sea.

But Europe cannot be defined in merely geographical terms. It does not have borders that separate it unambiguously from Asia. Europe is also a construction, subject to historical change. It can thus also be deconstructed. Today, Europe is deteriorating; it is becoming a purely economic construct.

Take the inhabitants of the Russian port of Vladivostok, which lies even further to the East than North Korea. Are they Europeans, and their neighbours Asians? A Japanese or Chinese person would only reluctantly call him- or herself an Asian.

If a German were to say to me 'You Asian!' it would sound like an insult, possibly even a racist slur. At the border between North Korea and Russia, if not somewhere even nearer, the concept of Europe becomes shaky.

The Germans have an inclination towards abstraction. It is very German, this question 'what is German?' No North Korean would ask the question 'what is North Korean?' The Koreans would answer 'kimchi or bibimbap'.[3]

The Germans, by contrast, will happily ruminate on the question 'what is German?' They will strive relentlessly to arrive at a definition, or invoke some sort of 'essence'.

In his 'On the Question: "What is German?"' Adorno also feels compelled to offer a definition. In his inimitable style he writes: 'It is in the faithfulness to the idea that the way things are should not be the final word – rather than in the hopeless attempt to determine finally what is German – that the sense this concept may still assert is to be surmised: in the transition to humanity.'[4]

Adorno elevates the 'German' such that it becomes a counter-image to the market and capitalism, contrasting it with the Americans, who, he says, have become the slaves of the market. To be German thus means to be committed to a form of humanity that radically breaks with capitalism.

Today, Europe is an abstract economic structure that steamrollers over the interests of its people. Europe fits neatly into the global. Everywhere, the economic abstraction of Europe creates discontent. Any abstraction leaves out differences. That is what constitutes its violence.

Globalization thus violently eliminates all regional differences in order to accelerate the circulation of capital and communication. The violence of this universal levelling awakens a longing for identity, and this longing is currently being satisfied mainly by right-wing populist parties.

The universal levelling effect of globalization – that is, the total monetarization of the world – deprives us of meaning and orientation. The de-siting violence of globalization awakens a longing for a site. Much like international terrorism, separatist and identitarian movements represent an irrational response to the violence of the levelling effects of the global. A terrorist is one who labours under the illusion that meaning can be created through coercion.

At present, Europe is merely an economic bureaucracy, a

free trade zone surrounded by walls and fences that guard it against any unwelcome guests. Globalization makes everything the same and everything comparable.

Anything foreign is pushed out. The singularity of the other irritates the global, which, in affirming itself, ignores us. The ascendancy of the global provokes reactive nationalisms, regionalisms and provincialisms, which present themselves as bearers of freedom and independence. Catalonia is an example of this.

Because of these developments, it is not desirable to be European. It is far better to remain German, and to seek inspiration elsewhere. It is more desirable to be French and be inspired by what is German than to be a homogeneous European.

At this year's Frankfurt Book Fair, the French president, Emmanuel Macron, remarked that he discovered Baudelaire through Walter Benjamin: a German, a German Jew, in other words, led a Frenchman to read Baudelaire. A foreigner deciphered his own culture for him.

The Frenchman is given a part of his own culture only through the mediation of a German, a German Jew. That means: what is foreign is constitutive of what is one's own. Without the foreign, we are blind to what is ours.

In 1964, the French singer Barbara, a French Jew, travelled to Göttingen and found inspiration in this foreign city. The result was a beautiful song, 'Göttingen', which won her worldwide fame. It was Barbara's ability to imagine the other that lent Göttingen its unmistakable identity. Barbara sings about the city as a place of love and reconciliation:

Of course, it's not the Seine
Nor the forest of Vincennes,
But a lot is to be said all the same
about Göttingen, about Göttingen.

About Paris there will always be songs,
But there are no songs about Göttingen,
And yet, love blossoms there as well
In Göttingen, in Göttingen.

According to Hegel, reconciliation is the mediation of the universal and the particular. If this is right, today's Europe is not a structure of reconciliation; it is a post-political, bureaucratic power that acts to oppose, or ignore, the particular.

Reconciliation also means freedom. If it is subordinated to the universal, the particular is unfree. The abstract universal provokes resistance of various kinds.

Speaking for myself, I do not necessarily want to make Germany my home. To me, Germany is a beautiful foreign place, and I am happy to remain a foreigner, inspired by a foreign place. I am a patriot, that is, a lover of the land: I love Germany as a foreign place, and German as a foreign language.

I also love foreign currencies. I am still irritated when I travel to Italy or France and find myself using the same currency. One of the pleasures of travel for me is that of taking a foreign banknote in my hand. The euro, everywhere the same, deprives me of that particular pleasure.

As a child, I was a passionate stamp collector. They stirred, in my imagination, thoughts of foreign lands. The prospect of European stamps fills me with horror. To me, foreign places have a seductive power. The same, the global, does not seduce or enchant me. I think the mind loves what is foreign. Without it, the well of inspiration dries up.

Barbara would not have aspired to become a European. She was a French Jew who sang her songs in both French and German out of a commitment to reconciliation. Barbara's German is beautiful. I cannot conceive of the beautiful apart from the foreign. All genuine beauty is foreign.

Global English, from which every trace of the foreign has been eliminated, is an utterly atrophied language. Germans talking to each other in global English sound bizarre. Germans should remain Germans. They should feel free to develop as many idiosyncrasies as they like, without feeling guilty about it.

The French should become not more European but more French – though without pledging allegiance to the Front National. The fact of our foreignness to one another is not something we should necessarily try to avoid. Today, we seek to eliminate foreignness because it prevents the global exchange of capital and information.

We claim a kind of authenticity for ourselves, but in truth we have become conformists. We have succumbed to the conformism of 'being different'.

If everyone were a European in the literal sense, that is, a human being with a broad view, peace on our planet might finally be possible. Another word for 'broad view' is reason. Europe can claim to be that cultural entity in which the concept of reason emerged.

The Enlightenment is a European achievement. But today we are increasingly leaving reason behind, taking refuge in the regressive mythologies of right-wing populism. Reason does not dictate that we build Fortress Europe but that we cultivate hospitality, as Immanuel Kant argued in his famous essay 'Perpetual Peace'.

At a time that is so dominated by hostility and enmity, it is worthwhile reminding oneself of this thought. Adorno might rather have said that to be a *European* means nothing other than to be 'in the transition to humanity'. Then I would love to be a European.

The Big Rush

From lack of repose our civilization is turning into a new barbarism. At no time have the active, that is to say the restless, counted for more. That is why one of the most necessary corrections to the character of mankind that has to be taken in hand is a considerable strengthening of the contemplative element in it.

Friedrich Nietzsche, *Human, All Too Human*[1]

Not all temporal forms can be accelerated. Attempting to accelerate a ritual act would be sacrilege. Rituals and ceremonies have their own time, their own rhythm and pace. All activities that are bound up with the seasons also resist acceleration. Caresses, prayers and processions cannot be accelerated. All narrative processes, and these include rituals and ceremonies, have their own time. Unlike counting, recounting does not admit of acceleration. Acceleration destroys the temporal structure of narration, the rhythm and pace of a narrative.

The speed of an electronic processor can be accelerated indefinitely because it works in a merely additive, not narrative, fashion. Thus, a processor differs from a procession; the latter is a narrative event. Today, we dispense with all ritual and ceremony, for they hinder the accelerating circulation of information, communication and capital. All temporal forms that fail to conform to the logic of efficiency are eliminated.

'Acceleration' is the name of the current temporal crisis. Everything is getting faster. Deceleration strategies are everywhere being proposed and praised, but the real temporal crisis consists in the fact that we have lost those temporal forms that cannot be accelerated, those temporal forms that allow us to experience duration. Today, labour time has become absolute: it represents time as such.

Labour time is that form of time that can be accelerated and exploited. Under present conditions, deceleration strategies are not about creating another form of time. Instead of transforming labour time into a different form of time, these strategies simply slow it down.

It is now scarcely even possible to experience duration. Labour time does not permit it. Labour time is not narrative time; it is an additive, even cumulative, time. This absence of duration creates the impression that everything is accelerating. The reason for duration's disappearance, however, is not, as is sometimes erroneously assumed, that everything is accelerating. Rather, it is precisely because time no longer has any hold [Halt], because nothing provides time with any duration, that time tumbles down, like an avalanche.[2] There is no longer any temporal attraction or tension between the point-like presences of which time now consists. They are purely additive. The result is the tearing away of time, a directionless, and hence meaningless, acceleration.[3]

Meaning founds duration. Our communication today is devoid of meaning; we communicate without interruption and without direction. A lapse in communication is like a death that must immediately be effaced through more communication. But this will always be a fruitless undertaking. Death cannot be eliminated by accelerated communication.

Our contemporary performance society takes time itself hostage by tying it to labour. The pressure to perform then becomes a pressure to accelerate. Labour as such is not necessarily destructive. It can bring about a 'deep but healthy tiredness', as Heidegger puts it.[4] But the pressure to perform produces a psychological pressure that can burn out the soul, even if the amount of work actually being carried out is not all that great. Burnout is a sickness caused not by work but by the pressure to perform. The soul is afflicted not because of work as such but because of performance, this new neoliberal principle.

The interruption of work we call a 'break' does not denote a different kind of time. It is only a phase within labour time. Today, all time is labour time. We have long since lost the time of the festival. The idea of 'calling it a day' [Feierabend] ahead of a festive day has become totally alien to us. The time of the festival is not a time of relaxation or recovery from work. A festival marks the beginning of an altogether different kind of time. The festival, like the celebration, belongs originally to a religious context. The Latin word *feriae* has a sacral origin, denoting the type of time proper to religious practice. *Fatum* means the holy place consecrated to the deity, that is, the place of worship dedicated to religious practice.

A festival begins where work, as 'pro-fane' (literally: situated before the sacred space) activity, ends. The time of the festival is the strict opposite of the time of work. Calling it a day ahead of a festive day means announcing the beginning of a period of holy time. Once we remove the border or threshold that separates the sacred and the profane, only the trivial and workaday remains: namely, pure labour time. Labour time is profaned time, time devoid of play or festival. And the imperatives of performance and efficiency exploit this sort of time.

Labour time is carried with us when we go on holiday; we even take it with us in our sleep. This is why our sleep is so restless today. Insofar as it serves the purpose of regenerating one's labour power, relaxation is just another mode of work. Seen in this light, relaxation is not the other of work; it is an expression of work. Taken by itself, deceleration, or slowness, cannot bring about a different kind of time. It is, in fact, a consequence of accelerated labour time. Deceleration cannot solve today's temporal crisis, as one commonly held view has it. Deceleration cannot heal, for it is a symptom, and you cannot heal an illness with one of its symptoms. Deceleration, taken by itself, does not turn work into festival.

What is needed today is not deceleration but a temporal revolution that inaugurates an altogether different kind of time. Acceleratable time is 'me time'. It is time that I take for myself. But there is also another form of time, the time of one's fellow human beings – the time I give to this fellow human being. The time of the other, as a kind of gift, cannot be accelerated. It also resists the imperatives of performance and efficiency. The temporal politics of neoliberalism has abolished this time of the other, the gift, completely. What is needed now is a different politics of time. Where 'me time' isolates and individualizes us, the time of the other inaugurates community, even shared time. That is *good* time.

In Your Face: How the Arts are Turning into Pornography. Or: On the Compulsion to Get Down to it, Without Seduction

Asked why he finally bade farewell to the theatre, Botho Strauß replied:

> I wanted to be an erotic author for the stage, but today pornographic authors – pornographic in the aesthetic or literal sense – dominate the theatres. I am interested in erotic connections and vicissitudes, but today connections and changes are no longer shown.[1]

And Thomas Ostermeier, in conversation, also identifies this change in the aesthetics of the theatre, describing the fundamental aesthetic rule of direction today as 'forestage, look at audience and shout' – that is, a *facial*, ejaculating into the audience.[2] Affects are produced and poured out over the audience. This pornographic and affect-based theatre has lost the quizzical or responsive gaze at the other. Connections and changes are no longer presented.

Erotic connections and vicissitudes require the other. We

increasingly experience the world from the perspective of the ego, and less and less from that of the other. Pornographic theatre lacks dialogue. It is, in Botho Strauß's words, an 'undertaking of private psychopathy'. The capacity for dialogue, the capacity to open up to the other, even the capacity to listen and respond, are atrophying. To stage a dialogue is not simply to stage a mutual exposure. Neither confessions nor disclosures are erotic. Unlike feeling, affect does not have a dialogical structure. It lacks the dimension of the other. There is therefore no such thing as 'com-emotion' [Mitemotion] or 'com-affect' [Mitaffekt]. Feelings are always com-passion [Mitgefühl].

An eroticist differs from a pornographer in that the former is indirect, takes detours. An eroticist is a lover of scenic distance. Instead of displaying something openly, he contents himself with allusion. An erotic actor is not a pornographic exhibitionist. Eroticism is allusive, not affective. The temporal mode of the pornographic, by contrast, is straight on. This is the trajectory of ejaculate. Deceleration and distraction are temporal modes of the erotic. Deixis, directly pointing at the thing, is pornographic. Pornography avoids detours.

In semiotic terms, the erotic arises from an excess of signifiers (signs), which circulate without being exhausted by their signified (meaning). This excess constitutes the secret and the seductive. A secret is not a hidden signified. It consists of a surplus that escapes meaning.

Today's turn towards the pornographic is not limited to the theatre. The imagery of porn extends to other areas. It colonizes perception itself, rendering it pornographic. We can no longer bear protraction, the long lasting, the quiet. We no longer have the patience for a long, slow narrative that spreads out through endless connections and vicissitudes. We are ruled by a pornographic compulsion, and it demands that we get down to business. The seductive gives way to the affective. We avoid allusion in favour of establishing direct links.

Digital tools for processing audio tracks include a setting called 'In your face'.[3] Applying it produces a more immediate, stronger sound. The sounds are poured directly into your face – again, a *facial*. The face is as it were drowned in sound.

Benedikt von Peter's new production of *Aida* at the Deutsche Oper Berlin exemplifies the turn towards the pornographic in music. *Aida* actually begins *pianissimo*. The first violins play *con sordino*, 'with muted strings'. When the second violins join in, also playing *con sordino*, the *pianissimo* becomes *pianississimo*: *ppp*. The music critic Christine Lemke-Matwey accuses von Peter's production of *Aida* of treating the quiet and intimate as a problem. In von Peter's production, everything is far too loud, brutally loud. The *pianissimi* are played *mezzo-forte*. During the triumphal march in the second act, she writes, one feels as though one's ear drums are about to burst. Another reviewer expresses it thus: 'It is so loud that the holes fly out of the cheese.' The overdriven sounds spill into the face – again, a *facial*.

In pornography, there is nothing to be deciphered. Jeff Koons once said that an observer of his works should only emit a simple 'wow'. His art, he added, does not require any judgement, interpretation or hermeneutics, no reflection or thought. It is emptied of all depths, all shallows. It simply offers itself up for consumption. Hans-Joachim Müller describes Koons's smooth sculptures as eliciting in the viewer a 'haptic compulsion' to touch them, even a desire to suck them. 'Wow': that is also the sound a porn actress would emit when confronted with an exposed, oversized penis, before beginning to suck it.

Jeff Koons's art lacks transcendence, which demands distance. It is the consumable immanence of the smooth that itself causes the haptic compulsion. It invites the observer to touch. The sense of touch 'is the most demystifying of all senses, unlike sight, which is the most magical'.[4] The sense of sight keeps a distance, while the sense of touch destroys distance. Without distance, there can be no mysticism. Demystification makes everything available for enjoyment and consumption. The sense of touch destroys the negativity of what is wholly other. It secularizes what it touches. In contrast to the sense of sight, touch is incapable of producing wonderment. The smooth touchscreen is thus a place of demystification and total consumption. The touchscreen exposes, demystifies, what is touched. In this sense, it is a pornographic apparatus. The same lack of distance we find in porn, with its endless touching and licking, is today found everywhere.

It is part of the aesthetics of contemporary film that the face is often shown in close-up. The body, body language, even language altogether, retreats from view. This muting of the body is pornographic. In a close-up, all the fragmented parts of a body appear as if they were sexual organs: 'The close-up of a face is as obscene as a close-up of a sexual organ.'[5]

What is beautiful is the object in its drapery, under its veil, in its hideout. Walter Benjamin therefore suggests that art criticism should be a *hermeneutics of veiling*: 'The task of art criticism is not to lift the veil but rather, through the most precise knowledge of it as a veil, to raise itself for the first time to the true view of the beautiful.'[6] Beauty conveys itself neither to direct empathy nor to naïve contemplation. Both are approaches that try to lift the veil, or to look through the veil. The only way to view beauty as a secret is through *knowledge of the veil itself*. In order to recognize what is veiled, one must first turn towards the veil. The veil is more essential than the veiled object.

According to Benjamin, Goethe's poetry is 'turned toward

the interior in the veiled light refracted through multicolored panes'. Goethe returned to the veil again and again when 'he was struggling for insight into beauty'.[7] Benjamin quotes from Goethe's *Faust*:

> Hold tight to what of all of it is left you
> The dress, don't let it go. Demons already
> Are tugging at the ends, would dearly like
> To haul it away to the underworld. Hold tight.
> It is no longer the goddess – you have lost her –
> But is divine.[8]

It is the dress that is divine. The veil is essential to beauty, so beauty cannot be undressed or unveiled. This impossibility of unveiling is the very nature of beauty.

Veiling also eroticizes texts. God, Augustine says, intentionally obscures the Holy Scripture through the use of metaphor, burying things 'under figures of speech'[9] in order to make them objects of desire. The *beautiful dress* of metaphor eroticizes the Scriptures. Dress is essential to the beautiful. The technique of veiling transforms hermeneutics into eroticism. It maximizes the *pleasure of the text* and turns reading into an act of love. The Torah also uses the technique of veiling. The text is represented as a lover hiding herself in a secret chamber within her palace, only for an instant unveiling her face to the one and only beloved, who himself remains hidden. Reading becomes an erotic adventure.

According to Roland Barthes, the erotic pleasure of a text differs from the 'pleasure of the corporeal striptease', which derives from a *progressive unveiling*.[10] A page-turner that builds and builds towards a final unveiling, a *final truth*, is also pornographic. The erotic can do *without truth*; it uses semblance.

Pornography – as nakedness without drapery, without secret – is the opposite of beauty. Its home is the shop window that 'shows only one illuminated piece of jewelry'. It 'is completely constituted by the presentation of only one thing: sex: no secondary, untimely object ever manages to half conceal, delay, or distract'.[11] Concealing, delaying and distracting are the spatio-temporal strategies of beauty. The strategy of semi-concealment is calculated to lend the beautiful a seductive lustre. The beautiful *hesitates* before appearing. Distraction protects it against direct contact. This is essential to eroticism. Pornography is without any distraction. It gets right down to it. Distraction transforms pornography into erotic photography. Thus Roland Barthes can write:

> A proof *a contrario*: Mapplethorpe shifts his close-ups of genitalia from the pornographic to the erotic by photographing the fabric of underwear at very close range: the photograph is no longer unary, since I am interested in the texture of the material.[12]

Unlike a pornographic picture, an erotic picture distracts us from the *object*. It makes the secondary object the main object, or subordinates the latter to the former. Beauty takes place beside the object [Sache], in the marginal [Nebensächliche]. There is no such thing as the *beautiful object*, nor is there such thing as a beautiful truth. 'Getting down to it' [Zur Sache selbst] is not a maxim of the arts.

The End of Liberalism:
The Coronavirus Pandemic and
Its Consequences

The threat of terrorism means we have grown accustomed to accepting, without protest, even the most humiliating security measures at airports. With hands in the air, we allow our bodies to be scanned. We allow ourselves to be searched for concealed weapons. Every one of us is a potential terrorist. The virus is a terror in the air. It represents a far graver threat than Islamist terrorism. It is almost a matter of the inexorable logic of the pandemic that society will be transformed into a permanent security zone, into a quarantine station in which everyone is treated as though they are infected.

In the course of the pandemic, Europe and the US have begun to lose their lustre. They are struggling. They seem not to be able to get a grip on the pandemic. By contrast, Asian countries such as Taiwan, Hong Kong, Singapore, South Korea and Japan have brought the pandemic under control relatively quickly. What is the reason for this? What systemic advantages do these Asian countries possess? The virus spreads easily in the liberal societies of Europe and the

US. Is liberalism, then, the reason for Europe's failure? Is the virus comfortable within the liberal system?

It will soon become clear that, in battling the pandemic, it is necessary to proceed at the micro-level, that is, to focus on individuals. But liberalism makes this difficult. A liberal society consists of individuals and their spaces of freedom, which the state is not allowed to access. Data protection alone is enough to prevent the surveillance of individuals at the micro-level. In a liberal society, the individual cannot be made the object of surveillance, so the only option is a complete shutdown, with all the serious economic implications this entails. A truly fateful insight will soon dawn on the West: that only a biopolitics that allows for unlimited access to the individual can prevent shutdowns, that it is exactly the protected private sphere which provides the protected space for the virus. This insight, however, spells the end of liberalism.

The Asians have dealt with the virus with a rigour and discipline that is unimaginable to Europeans. The individual is the focus of surveillance; that is the main difference from the European fight against the pandemic. The rigorous measures implemented in Asia are reminiscent of the disciplinary measures implemented during the Great Plague in seventeenth-century Europe. Michel Foucault provided an impressive description of these measures in his analysis of the disciplinary society. Houses were locked from the outside, and the keys handed to the authorities. The penalty for those who tried to escape quarantine was death. Stray animals were killed. The surveillance was total, and absolute obedience was demanded. Houses were checked one by one, with inhabitants having to appear at a window. Those who lived at the rear of a house and did not have a window facing the street were allocated one. Names were read out, and everyone was asked to report their state of health. Those who lied faced the death penalty. A comprehensive registration system was created. Space congealed into a network of impermeable cells. Everyone was tied to their place. Those who moved risked their lives.

In the seventeenth century, Europe developed into a disciplinary society. Biopolitical power crept into the most trivial aspects of life. Society as a whole was transformed into a panopticon; it was permeated by the panoptical gaze. The memory of these disciplinary measures has completely faded. In fact, they went much further than the measures adopted by China in the face of the pandemic. But, one might say, the Europe of the seventeenth and eighteenth centuries is not the China of today. China has created a digital disciplinary society. It has a social-scoring system that makes possible the complete biopolitical surveillance and control of the population. No aspect of everyday life remains unobserved. Each click, each purchase, each contact, each activity on social media is subject to surveillance. There are 200 million surveillance cameras with facial recognition technology in operation. Those who drive through a red light, meet up with people who oppose the regime, or post critical comments on social media live dangerously. But those who buy healthy food or read newspapers loyal to the party are rewarded with easy credit, cheaper health insurance, or travel permits. Such comprehensive surveillance is possible in China because internet and mobile phone providers pass on all of their data to the authorities. The state thus knows where I am, who I am meeting, what I am doing, what I am looking for, what I am thinking, what I am buying, what I am eating. It is conceivable that, in the future, body temperature, weight, blood sugar levels, etc., will also be controlled by the state.

This comprehensive digital surveillance of the population has proved to be highly effective in fighting the virus. When you leave the train station in Beijing, you are captured by a camera that registers your body temperature. If it turns out that you have a fever, the people who were sitting in the same train carriage are automatically informed via their mobile phones – the system knows, of course, where everyone was sitting. There are even reports on social media of drones being used to enforce quarantine. If someone attempts to slip out of their apartment, a drone approaches to instruct the person to return home. Perhaps the drone could one day even print a fine and deliver it into the person's hands – who knows? In the battle against the pandemic, a paradigm shift seems to be taking place, one that has not been sufficiently appreciated by the West: it is being digitalized. The pandemic is being fought not only by virologists and epidemiologists but, in large part, by IT and Big Data specialists.

In the battle against the virus, the individual is under surveillance as an individual. There is an app that allocates a coloured QR code to every individual, indicating their state of health. Red means two weeks of quarantine. Only those with a green code are allowed to move freely. And it is not only China; other Asian countries have also banked on individual surveillance. A variety of data is collated in order to detect those who might be infected. The South Korean government is even considering making it compulsory for people in quarantine to wear digital bracelets that would allow them to be monitored around the clock, a kind of surveillance that was previously used only for sex offenders. In the pandemic everyone is treated like a potential criminal.

The Asian model of how to fight the virus is not compatible with Western liberalism. The pandemic has revealed the cultural differences between Asia and Europe. In Asia, we still have a disciplinary society, a collectivism with a strong tendency towards discipline. Radical disciplinary measures that would be roundly rejected by Europeans can be easily implemented. They are experienced not as infringements of individual rights but as the fulfilment of collective duties. Countries like China or Singapore are autocratic regimes.

And it was only a few decades ago that South Korea and Taiwan were autocratic regimes too. Authoritarian regimes teach the people to be obedient disciplinary subjects. And Asia is formed by Confucianism, which demands absolute obedience to authority. All these peculiarities of Asian culture turn out to be systemic advantages when it comes to containing the virus. Does this mean the Asian form of disciplinary society will prevail as the pandemic continues?

But we do not need to refer to Asia to point out the dangers the pandemic has created for Western liberalism. Panoptical surveillance is not an exclusively Asian phenomenon. We are all already living in a global digital panopticon. Social media increasingly resembles a panopticon that monitors and ruthlessly exploits its users. We expose ourselves voluntarily. The disclosure of data is not coerced; it follows from an inner need. We are constantly asked to share our opinions, preferences and needs – to tell our life story. This data then becomes the object of ruthless commercial exploitation by the digital platforms, which use it to predict and manipulate our behaviour.

We live under a digital feudalism. The digital feudal lords, like Facebook, give us some land and say: 'You can have it for free. Cultivate it.' And we cultivate it exhaustively. At the end of it all, our feudal lords return for the harvest. This is a surveillance and exploitation of all communication. The system is extremely efficient. No one protests against it, because the system exploits freedom itself.

Surveillance capitalism transforms capitalism itself. Platforms such as Google, Facebook and Amazon constantly monitor and manipulate us in order to maximize their profits. Every click is registered and analysed. We are controlled like puppets on algorithmic strings. At the same time, we feel free. There is a dialectics of freedom here: freedom turns into serfdom. Is this still a form of liberalism?

At this point, we need to ask: Given that this digital surveillance machinery is already up and running, why should it stop short of the virus? It is likely that the pandemic will break down the psychological barrier which has hitherto prevented the biopolitical expansion of surveillance into the sphere of the individual. Because of the pandemic, we are heading towards a biopolitical regime of surveillance. Digital surveillance will monitor not only our communication but also our bodies, our state of health. The digital surveillance society will undergo a biopolitical expansion.

According to Naomi Klein, the moment of shock is the perfect time to establish a new system of rule. The shock of the pandemic will ensure that a digital biopolitics, a biopolitical disciplinary society, will prevail at the global level. It will take hold of our bodies and constantly monitor our state of health. What is more, it is quite possible that, within this biopolitical surveillance regime, we will feel free. After all, we might say, all these surveillance measures are only in the interests of our own health. Domination comes into its own at the point where it coincides with freedom. Amid the shock of the pandemic, will the West feel forced to abandon its liberal principles? Are we threatened by the imminent emergence of a biopolitical quarantine society that will place enduring limits on our freedom? In other words: is China Europe's future?

CONVERSATIONS

It Is Eros That Defeats Depression

A Conversation with Ronald Düker and Wolfram Eilenberger

Philosophie Magazin: Let us first talk about your background, because it is rather unusual. What attracts someone from South Korea to Germany? Why does a student of metallurgy become a philosopher?

Byung-Chul Han: There are certain ruptures and transformations in one's life that cannot be explained. I may have taken this unusual decision because of my name. Adorno once said names are initials that we do not understand but that we obey. The Chinese sign for 'Chul', when spoken, means both 'iron' and 'light'. In Korean, philosophy is the 'science of light'. I may have thus just been following my name.

PM: To Germany . . .

BCH: Yes, I came to Germany after having been accepted to study metallurgy at the Technische Hochschule Clausthal Zellerfeld, near Göttingen. I told my parents that I would continue to study for my technology degree in Germany. I had to lie to them. Otherwise, they would not have let me go. I simply set off, to an altogether different country, whose language I could neither speak nor write, and I plunged into the study of an altogether different discipline. It was as in a dream. I was twenty-two at the time.

PM: Your book *The Burnout Society* was a bestseller in Germany, and has now also attracted a cult following in South Korea. How do you explain its success?

BCH: That's true – it sold as many copies there as Stéphane Hessel's *Time for Outrage!* sold in Germany. Apparently, the central thesis of the book – that today's performance society is a society of self-exploitation, and that exploitation now takes place even without domination – appealed to the Koreans. South Korea is a burnout society in the final stages of the syndrome. In fact, everywhere in Korea you can see people sleeping. Subway trains in Seoul look like sleeper cars.

PM: And that used to be different?

BCH: When I was at school, there were slogans displayed on the classroom wall praising concepts such as patience, diligence and so on: the classic slogans of a disciplinary society. But today the country has been transformed into a performance society, and this transformation took place more rapidly and more brutally than elsewhere. No one was given time to prepare for neoliberalism, the most extreme version of the performance society. Suddenly, everything is about 'skills' and being-able-to-do, and no longer about what you must or should do. The classrooms are now filled with slogans like 'yes you can!' My book seems to have been something of an antidote to this situation. Maybe its success heralds a more critical consciousness, albeit one that is only just beginning to emerge.

PM: What is the basic problem with the neoliberal ethics of performance?

BCH: The problem is that it is so cunning, and therefore so devastatingly efficient. Let me explain this. Karl Marx criticized a society in which external domination ruled. Under capitalism, the worker is exploited by others, and this external exploitation, given a certain level of production, reaches a limit. The self-exploitation to which we submit ourselves today is very different. Self-exploitation is limitless! We voluntarily exploit ourselves until we break down. If I fail, I take responsibility for this failure. If I suffer, if I go bust, I have only myself to blame. Because it is wholly voluntary, self-exploitation is exploitation without domination. And because it takes place under the guise of freedom, it is highly efficient. There is no emerging collective, no 'we', that could rise up against the system.

PM: Your diagnosis of our society's ills deploys the unusual conceptual pair of positivity and negativity. You find that negativity is disappearing. What is the purpose of negativity? And what do you mean by 'negativity' in the first place?

BCH: Negativity is something that triggers a defensive immunological response. The other is a negativity that seeks to penetrate into oneself, and seeks to negate, to destroy you. I have claimed that we are currently living in a post-immunological age. Today's psychological illnesses, such as

95

depression, ADHD or burnout, are not infections caused by viral or bacterial negativity but infarctions caused by an excess of positivity. Violence is not only caused by negativity but also by positivity – not only by the other but also by the same. The violence of positivity, or the same, is a post-immunological violence. What makes us ill is the obesity of the system. As we know, there is no immunological reaction to fat.

PM: In what sense is depression related to the disappearance of negativity?

BCH: Depression is a consequence of a pathologically intensified narcissistic relation to the self. Those suffering from depression sink and drown in themselves. They have lost the other. Have you seen Lars von Trier's film *Melancholia*? The protagonist, Justine, is an illustration of what I'm saying: she is a depressive because she is totally exhausted, worn down by herself. All of her libido is directed at her own subjectivity, and she is therefore incapable of love. And then – well, then a planet appears, the planet Melancholia. In the hell of the same, the arrival of what is wholly other can take the form of the apocalypse. The death-dealing planet reveals itself to Justine as the wholly other, which wrests her out of her narcissistic swamp. In the face of this death-dealing planet, she flourishes. She discovers others. She begins to care for Claire and her son, for example. The planet sparks erotic desire. Eros, the relation to the wholly other, cures depression. The disaster carries salvation within it. The word 'disaster', incidentally, comes from the Latin *desastrum*, meaning 'unlucky star'. 'Melancholia' is an unlucky star.

PM: You want to say: only a disaster can save us?[1]

96

BCH: We live in a society that is fully geared towards production, fully geared towards positivity. This society abolishes the negativity of the other, or of the foreign, in order to accelerate the cycle of production and consumption. The only differences that are permitted are those that can be consumed. An other whose otherness has been taken away cannot be loved, only consumed. This is perhaps why there is a renewed interest in the apocalypse. We are aware of a hell of the same from which we wish to escape.

PM: Could you possibly offer us a catchier definition of 'the other'?

BCH: The other is also the object [Gegenstand]; it is even decency [Anstand]. We have lost the capacity, the decency, to see the other in its otherness, because we flood everything with our intimacy. The other is something that questions me, that wrests me from my narcissistic inwardness.

PM: But are we not in fact witnessing the formation of a resisting 'we' in, for instance, recent protest movements like Occupy – a 'we' that sees the system, here represented by the stock exchange and markets, as an other that it wants to attack?

BCH: That is not enough. A stock market crash isn't quite an apocalypse. It is a problem internal to the system, and it has to be resolved quickly. And what difference do 300 or 400 people, quickly carted away by the police, make here? This is not even close to the kind of 'we' that we would need. The apocalypse is an atopical event. It comes from an altogether different place.

PM: What, then, is the way out?

BCH: A society without the other is a society without Eros. Literature, art and poetry also live off the desire for the wholly other. The current crisis in the arts is perhaps also a crisis of love. Soon – I am certain about this – we will no longer understand the poems of Paul Celan, because they are addressed to the wholly other. The new media of communication abolish the other. One of Celan's poems reads: 'You are so close, as if you were not lingering here.' This is what it is about! Absence: that is the fundamental trait of the other; that is negativity. Because he does not linger here, I am able to speak. Only for that reason is poetry possible. Eros aims at the wholly other.

PM: That would make love utopian, something that cannot possibly be realized.

BCH: Desire is fuelled by the impossible. But if the constant message, for instance in advertising, is 'you can' and 'everything is possible', then this marks the end of erotic desire. There is no love any longer because we imagine ourselves to be utterly free, because we have too many options to choose from. Of course, the other is your enemy. But the other is also your lover. It is like mediaeval courtly love: as Jacques Lacan said, it is like a black hole around which desire condenses. We are no longer familiar with this hole.

PM: Haven't we replaced a belief in transcendence with a belief in transparency? Hardly anything else matters any more, especially in politics.

BCH: Yes, secrets are a negativity. They are characterized by a withdrawal. Transcendence is also a negativity, while immanence is a positivity. Thus, the excess of positivity appears in the form of the terror of immanence. The transparency society is a society of positivity.

PM: How do you explain the cult of transparency?

BCH: First of all, it is important to understand the digital paradigm. I consider the introduction of digital technologies to be a historical turning point as dramatic as the invention of writing or the printing press. The digital as such pushes us towards transparency. When I push a button on the computer I immediately get a result. The temporality of the transparency society is immediacy, real time. Any logjam, any logjam in the flow of information, is no longer tolerated. Everything must be immediately visible in the present.

PM: The Pirate Party believes that this immediacy can improve our politics.

BCH: 'Liquid feedback', I think, is the magic phrase in this context. It is as though representative democracy created an unbearable temporal logjam. But this idea leads to massive problems, because there are things that cannot be done immediately, things that first need to mature. And politics should be an experiment, an experiment where the outcome is open. As long as experimentation is ongoing, the result cannot be known. If one is implementing a vision, one actually needs a temporal logjam. What the Pirate Party envisages is therefore a politics without vision. And the same holds true at the level of the corporation. Everything is being endlessly evaluated. An optimal result must be achieved every day. It is no longer possible to pursue long-term projects. The digital habitus also involves us in constantly changing our positions. Politicians will therefore cease to exist, for a politician is someone who insists on a certain position.

PM: And you take all this to be the result of the new technology?

BCH: Well, what does 'digital' actually mean? Digital is derived from *digitus*, the Latin word for finger. In the context of the digital, human activity is reduced to the activity of the fingertips. But it is worth remembering that human activity was traditionally associated with the hand – hence the terms 'Handlung' [act], 'handicraft'. Today, all we do is twiddle our fingers. This is the lightness of digital being. An action in the true sense, however, is always a kind of drama. Heidegger's fetishization of the hand was already a protest against the digital.

PM: This question of whether it is even still possible to act and experiment also has something to do with the fact that, in this new digital logic, there are no longer any leadership figures – that it is a politics without leaders.

BCH: That is already the case with the Pirate Party. Leadership is a distinctive activity. If you want to lead, you must keep your eyes on the future. A leader is someone who looks into the future. And if I embark on a political experiment, I must be able to take a risk, because the result will not immediately be available to me, because I enter a space of incalculability. Leaders, in the sense of a vanguard, enter the realm of the incalculable. The transparency associated with the digital, by contrast, strives for total calculability. Everything must be calculable. But actions cannot be calculated. Otherwise, they would be mere calculation. Acting always touches upon the incalculable, reaches into the future. That means the transparency society is a society without a future. Future is the temporal dimension of the wholly other. Today, the future is just the optimized present.

PM: Is the celebration of immediacy not also a kind of infantilization? Three-year-olds also cannot bear it when their parents do not immediately give them what they want.

BCH: Of course. The digital infantilizes us because it makes it that we are no longer able to wait. For instance, think about how the temporality of love is being lost. The sentence 'I love you' is, after all, a kind of promise that binds me in the future. Today, all those human acts that explicitly aim at the future, such as taking responsibility or making promises, are withering away. The temporal horizon of knowledge, insight or experience [Erfahrung] is also the future. The temporality of information or lived experience [Erlebnis], by contrast, is the present. The information society has produced a new illness: it is called information fatigue syndrome. One of its symptoms is a paralysis of our analytical capacities. Deluged by information, we are now apparently incapable of distinguishing between what is important and what is not. Interestingly, another symptom of this condition is an inability to take responsibility.

PM: You have also called the transparency society a 'porn society'. Why?

BCH: The transparency society is a porn society in that it involves the totalization and absolutization of visibility. We no longer have any sense of that which is concealed. Because it renders everything a commodity and puts everything on show, capitalism intensifies this development towards the pornographic in our society. The goal is maximum exhibition value. Capitalism knows of no other way of making use of sexuality. But erotic tension does not result from the permanent display of nudity but from a staged alternation of fading in and fading out. It is the negativity of interruption that makes nudity erotic.

PM: So the pornographic destroys the erotic.

BCH: Yes. Think of that wonderful moment in *Madame Bovary*: the coach ride of Leon and Emma – an aimless carriage ride around the whole city, with the reader not learning anything about what goes on inside the coach. Instead, Flaubert lists squares and streets. In the end, Emma stretches her hand out of the window and releases shreds of paper that float like butterflies onto a field of clover. Her hand is the only thing that is naked in the scene. It is the most erotic moment imaginable, because you see nothing. The conditions of hypervisibility in which we live make something like this inconceivable.

PM: What is philosophy's role amid this hell of the same?

BCH: For me, philosophy is an attempt at imagining an altogether different form of life. It is about putting different life plans to the test, at least intellectually. Aristotle showed us how it is done. He invented the *vita contemplativa*. Today, philosophy is far from this. It has become part of the hell of the same. In a letter, Heidegger once compared thinking to Eros. He spoke of the flapping of Eros's wings carrying him to untrodden paths. Perhaps philosophy is the caress that inscribes forms and linguistic patterns into the skin of the mute other.

PM: You are now a professor, but your relationship with academic philosophy has not always been so harmonious, has it?

BCH: As you know, I am a professor of philosophy at an arts college. I am probably too lively for a philosophy department at a university. Unfortunately, academic philosophy in Germany is totally moribund and lifeless. It does not seek to address the present or the social problems of the present.

PM: What should it be addressing, what challenges our thinking?

BCH: Today, there are so many things and events that call for philosophical elaboration. For me, depression, transparency or even the Pirate Party are philosophical problems. In particular, digitalization and digital connectivity present philosophy with important tasks and challenges. We need a new digital anthropology, a digital theory of knowledge and perception. We need a digital social philosophy and philosophy of culture. A digital reboot of Heidegger's *Being and Time* is long overdue.

PM: What do you mean by that?

BCH: Heidegger replaced the subject with Dasein [existence or being-there]. We now have to replace the subject with the project. We are no longer 'thrown' [geworfen]. We have no 'fate'. We are designing [entwerfende] projects. Digitalization spells the end of Heidegger's 'thing'. It creates a new kind of being and a new kind of time. We need to take greater theoretical risks. Academic philosophy is too cautious for that. I wish it was more courageous and daring. 'Spirit' [Geist] originally meant agitation or emotion [Ergriffenheit]. In that sense, academic philosophy is spiritless.

Capitalism Dislikes Silence

A Conversation with Thomas Ostermeier and Florian Borchmeyer

Thomas Ostermeier: Is greed at the root of the problems in the unfettered financial markets?

Byung-Chul Han: You cannot explain capitalism on the basis of greed alone. I have come to believe that what is at work here is the death drive. Maybe we are wrecking ourselves, destroying in order to grow. There is no renewal. When people talk about 'renewal', it is really an attempt to make things seem old and obsolete as soon as possible – an engine of destruction, really. Today, things are stillborn. War breaks out at that point where, because of a lack of new markets, the burgeoning productive forces explode and are discharged in an unnatural way. Consumption destroys things in a natural way. We consume in the interests of peace [laughs]. Not only the destruction of nature but also intellectual destruction . . .

TO: . . . and personal destruction. What you describe in *The Burnout Society* is also a destruction of the human psyche . . .

BCH: . . . yes, and that is why I say this is the death drive . . .

Florian Borchmeyer: Perhaps it is not just about greed but about longing. Capitalism is a system that generates desires that previously did not exist at all – new desires and longings – and so people invent new products that no one had any need for before.

BCH: Eva Illouz connects capitalism with romanticism, with consumerist romanticism. But I am not sure whether capitalism is romantic. Longing relates to the impossible, to what is out of reach. The object of longing cannot be an object of consumption. What happens is the opposite: longing is destroyed. Who today suffers amorous longing? Love itself consists of consumable feelings. Capitalism constantly produces consumer needs. You do not feel a longing for a new smartphone; the internet is not a space of longing.

TO: In your book, you say that capitalism is not a religion – it does not allow debt repayment [Entschuldung] or expiation.[1]

BCH: Yes, I did say that. In particular, I was arguing against Walter Benjamin, who said that capitalism is a cult that does not expiate sins but leads only to indebtedness. But an essential part of religion is atonement [Entschuldung] and expiation; there can be no religion without salvation. Capitalism produces only indebtedness. It may be that human beings accrue debt in order not to be free. If you are free, you must act. People point to their guilt or debt in order to avoid having to act. And, yes, Max Weber also connects capitalism with the possibility of salvation.

TO: What does salvation mean in capitalism?

BCH: Not everyone is a chosen one. And you do not know whether you are one of the chosen ones. If I am successful, if I accumulate capital, then I am one of the chosen ones.

TO: Calvinism . . . But capitalism does not promise salvation in an afterlife, only here.

BCH: If I earn ten million euros a year, that is an instance of the sublime.

TO: But not of redemption.

BCH: The semblance of redemption. If I possess this kind of wealth, I have the illusion of omnipotence and immortality. Wealth [Vermögen] – what a beautiful word.[2] Infinite wealth means infinite capacity; finitude fades away. What is salvation? This illusion is surely enough. There is a very theological dimension to it, and that dimension has nothing to do with material greed. There are many shades of the death drive in capitalism. We destroy so much! Everybody knows that things today are stillborn.

TO: Let us change tack and talk about love, then. The theatre is in the middle of a major crisis because we are unable to convey feelings on the stage.

BCH: Why does the theatre necessarily need feelings?

TO: Because it describes emotions.

BCH: If you can describe a situation, then the emotions will emerge; feelings will be produced. I play a character, without emotion. I make a gesture. And that gesture may overwhelm the audience. If I create a character, a gesture, it produces a narration. Narrations create feelings. If a narration tries to express feelings directly, then the result is porn, as Botho Strauß would say. Theatre today, he says, is pornography. It lacks the erotic. The actors are all psychopaths. On his telling, there has been a fundamental degeneration in theatre.

TO: And what should be narrated?

BCH: Acts!

TO: Of course. But there is also that moment where the action creates in the spectator a state of catharsis, to use a very old term: a moment of emotional cleansing that results from the emotional experience prompted by the action on stage.

BCH: Feelings are always coded. And in the theatre it was always the case – even as early as the eighteenth century – that society confirms the code. And within the framework of this code, feelings arise. Feelings are confirmations of this code.

FB: Maybe we should not focus so exclusively on the narration of feeling, because the feelings are not what is being narrated as the topic of a play – the feelings are the driving forces in the play . . .

BCH: But that is very interesting!

FB: . . . feelings do not constitute the plot as such. Otherwise, you would indeed quickly end up with porn, if you wanted to produce a play about a feeling, a play about love that would explain or exhibit love. But, still, feelings have always been, ever since the Greek tragedians, the driving forces of every dramatic plot. In *Antigone*, feelings may not be the theme, but they are the driving force.

TO: What motivates action is always the difference between the place where a character finds himself and where he would like to be. That is why a character chooses to act.

FB: And that triggers, according to Aristotle, fear and pity, which are, of course, emotional categories.

BCH: Mr Ostermeier, you said the theatre's current crisis is caused by the inability to narrate feeling. Why is this a crisis today? Was it different before?

TO: It was different before because feelings were not frowned upon, because there were feelings and words that corresponded to them. But today, as you describe in your book, we have been deprived of Eros because we have been deprived of the other.

BCH: Emotions are frowned upon today? Why?

TO: At least this is the case in the theatre. Feelings such as pity, grief, empathy, affection, devotion are frowned upon . . .

FB: . . . at least their direct display . . .

TO: When I go to the theatre, the basic emotion conveyed to me from the stage is, usually, aggression – in-your-face aggression. I always ask myself: why is this person incessantly shouting at me? I didn't do anything to him.

BCH: I see . . . I was at the theatre recently. It was too loud. I found it irritating, annoying. I left at the interval. I wanted more a theatre of stillness, where there is only whispering. Why is there so much shouting?

TO: I often ask myself the same question. Is it simply a consequence of the fact that we no longer have the right instruments at our disposal? Could the instruments be lacking not because theatre would be in a crisis, but because theatre can only ever be as good as the society it reflects. And a society that only ever shouts or is mute will have a theatre that only shouts or no longer exists. What might be the answer to the question about the crisis of feeling?

BCH: To begin with, we need a conceptual clarification. Feeling and emotion are altogether different things. Feeling is altogether different from affect. Your questions contain a conceptual vagueness in this respect. If we are to discuss these matters, we need conceptual clarity. You may talk of the feeling of beauty. But you cannot say: emotion of beauty or affect of beauty. And from the linguistic expression alone you can deduce what an enormous difference there is between feeling and affect. A 'feel for the ball' in football, for instance. An affect for the ball? An emotion for the ball? [laughs]. Or a feeling for language. A feeling is a state or a faculty, something static. And emotion is always *émouvoir*: an emotion may thus trigger an action. We can put it this way: we find ourselves in a crisis of feeling because of the rise of affect. 'Why do they shout so much on stage?' you just asked. They act on the basis of affect, not with feeling. Feelings are intersubjective. Feelings found community, meaning they are something social. An affect can be something very anti-social, something that separates or is separated.

TO: Is anger an affect or a feeling?

BCH: That depends on the context. You cannot sing an affect. Narrating feelings means singing them. There is singing in theatres. For singing you need a narrative structure, a narrative space. It therefore depends on what you mean by anger. Take 'wrath', the first word of the Iliad.

FB: The story of wrath. 'Achilles' wrath . . . heavenly goddess sing!' . . .

BCH: The very first drama of European culture begins with wrath. 'Menin'. Singing wrath. Wrath that can be sung is not a simple affect but something that is carried by the whole community, that causes the whole course of the action.

FB: The wrath that is being narrated goes beyond the individual wrath of Achilles . . .

BCH: Of course!

FB: . . . that puts in question a whole social system, and beyond that even the world of the gods, because the Iliad tells the story of the Trojan War from beginning to end. The beginning of the drama lies in Achilles' wrath arising, and once that wrath is appeased the drama also ends. This makes the feeling of wrath a dramatic feeling.

BCH: This wrath can be sung, meaning: it can be narrated. And the problem in this drama is not the question 'how can there be stories about feelings?' The drama consists of the narration of this one feeling: wrath. You can only understand the crisis of feeling if you distinguish feeling from affect. If you want to create feeling, you need to open up a resonating space. This is not the case with affects. They are like projectiles. Affects seek out their path; they cannot open up a space.

TO: Based on your knowledge of the history of the human mind [Geistesgeschichte], do you think there are certain feelings that are in the process of disappearing, and others that are on the rise? Or is it simply that feelings are shrinking and affects growing?

BCH: I think that feelings are spaces that cannot be consumed. But emotions and affects can become consumable.

TO: [whispers] Feelings as well!

BCH: Feelings cannot be consumed. You cannot consume grief. You cannot earn money from grief. Today, there are 'angry citizens' [Wutbürger] and waves of indignation.[3] But is such indignation wrath? Wrath can be sung. Indignation, this shitstorm, cannot be sung. Indignation is something subjective and separate.

TO: But what about the *Indignados* in Spain?

BCH: The *Indignados*, in fact the whole Occupy movement, have fizzled out.

TO: Why?

BCH: This system isolates people. How can a 'we' emerge in a system where everyone is on their own? Everything is fleeting.

TO: But, at the same time, we keep hearing about how today's businesses seek to create familial feelings. Businesses try to connect with employees emotionally in order to make them more exploitable. . . . It used to be that a factory worker knew: 'my boss is exploiting me, but I have no choice because I have to feed my five children'. But now we have a situation, as you

111

have also described in your book *The Burnout Society*, of self-exploitation. And that starts as soon as I say: 'my business, the place I work, is my family, my home, the place where I am also emotionally cared for'.

BCH: Capitalism economizes feelings. If I were strictly rational about shopping, I would not buy much. You have to mobilize emotion in order to produce more needs.

FB: Emotions or feelings?

BCH: Emotions! Emotion is a movement that moves me to reach for something. Emotions are highly unstable; rationality is very stable. I may hold on to my convictions, but emotions fluctuate. In order to increase turnover and create new needs, capitalism requires more than just rationality. That is why capitalism has discovered the usefulness of emotion in connection with consumption. Advertisements must stir emotions; then purchases will follow. Consumption will outstrip rational need. The power of emotion has also been discovered at the level of management. Emotional leadership goes much deeper, and thus allows for a more comprehensive exploitation. The feeling of freedom that says 'you do not work for someone else; you are optimizing yourself; you are your own project' follows the same logic as 'I am part of a family; I develop and flourish' . . .

TO: . . . 'I carry out a project' . . .

BCH: . . . and initiative . . . coming from inside of me. That is obviously much more efficient than exploitation from outside. Emotions allow for the creation of internal fetters, and those are even worse than the external ones.

TO: Affects on the rise at the expense of feelings. Could we go so far as to say, as you already hinted, that the more we lose our community, the more we shall also lose our feelings?

BCH: Botho Strauß says: 'Just a moment ago, we heard the silvery, almost singing tone of a girl, and the very next instant it was lowered abruptly by an interval and has become a guttural, almost rattling, sometimes actually vulgar sound. The fast-changing voice is not coloratura but a dialogical binding force: wanting to find out something about the other, and together with him.'[4]

For Botho Strauß, theatre is a dialogical space, and only in that space do we find Eros – in this attempt at getting closer to the other.

TO: This has been my main theme during rehearsals over the last two years. I only discovered this theme for myself because of a deep frustration with the acting, because I said 'stop wanting to produce feelings all by yourself'.

It used to be that there was a looking at the other. I do not know whether they really played together back then, but at least they looked at each other and had an aesthetic code . . . And they tried to experience the other actors, to understand or to convince them. In today's art of theatre directing, the fundamental aesthetic rule is: 'forestage, look at the audience and shout'. Something that was once a revolutionary act has thus become an aesthetically trivial, empty gesture, because it is no longer revolutionary. It only repeats old patterns.

BCH: If you want to talk about feelings, you first have to learn how to play with each other. If you play together, there will be narration.

TO: That is exactly what I do in my rehearsals. I tell the actors: 'stop approaching what you do like craftsmen, and think "this is the outline of the character; now I shall fill it in with my brush"'.

BCH: The theatre is becoming noisy. I still feel at ease in Japanese theatres, Noh theatre, Kabuki theatre. I do not find these as irritating. I like to go to the cinema. When I go to the theatre, I am annoyed by the actors [laughs].

TO: . . . because the actors only have one feeling left: they want to irritate you. It's stupid. The noisiness of the theatre signals that society that has lost a sense for feelings as social phenomena. But since we still want theatre to elicit feelings, we act with affect, in order to provoke.

BCH: Provoke?

TO: Yes, our affects provoke an emotion in the audience.

BCH: Affects cannot really produce feelings.

TO: No, actually, counter-affects. Affects provoke exactly what you just mentioned: it is too noisy! That was your reaction – and that is nothing but an affect, right?

BCH: No, it was noisy. There was no narrative tension.

TO: Narrative tension has fallen into disrepute!

BCH: Only narrative tension can create feeling.

TO: But when we have a theatre culture dominated by the idea of the 'post-dramatic', how is that supposed to work?

BCH: But what does 'post-dramatic' mean?

FB: Situations instead of plots.

TO: 'Post-dramatic' means: in a world in which narration has become impossible, because you can no longer identify subjects who act, you can no longer construct a dramatic plot. Your experience of the world is completely chaotic. You do not know who is responsible for what. And that is the world you are trying to reflect, and it can only be reflected in post-dramatic fashion.

BCH: But you can try to present an alternative vision.

TO: The kind of theatre I make is a sort of desperate attempt to create an alternative vision.

BCH: But we should not just repeat what we have long since left behind; rather, we should invent a new form of narration.

TO: That form is dramatic. The tension of narration produces feeling. But in order to do that I need a dramatic plot.

BCH: I am not sure whether narration always has to be dramatic.

TO: No, it doesn't. Novels also work.

FB: Exactly, and maybe we need to move even further away from theatre. In *The Agony of Eros* you write: 'Today, love is being positivized into a formula for enjoyment. Above all, love is supposed to generate pleasant feelings. It no longer represents plot, narration, or drama – only inconsequential emotion and arousal.'[5] So far, we have approached this theme in the context of theatre. But the theme seems just to mirror what is going on in society.

BCH: Love also has a plot. Love today is simply an arrangement of pleasant, consumable feelings. Faithfulness is not an emotion; faithfulness is an act. Determination. Faithfulness turns chance into fate. It creates eternity.

TO: Most people today think of love as a bubble bath.[6]

BCH: A roller-coaster of affects [Wechselbad von Affekten]. And that is why people constantly change partners, because people are hungry for fresh affects, fresh experiences of affect. So love becomes unstable.

TO: What would be your solution to this problem of the satisfaction of affect through the constant changing of partners?

BCH: It is the result of love no longer having a plot. Gorz's *Letter to D*, a French philosopher's letter to his wife, presents us with an avowal of faithfulness. He says something like: 'You're 85 years old and have shrunk five centimetres. You only weigh 40 kilos now, yet you're still desirable.'[7] This faithfulness has a plot. Faithfulness does not simply come about as a feeling.

TO: But there are still affects that intervene, such as, 'oh dear, how do I know this person is the person I love and with whom I want to follow the plot of love and the plot of faithfulness for all of my life? How do I know it's not one of those other eight people I could also get?'

BCH: We are living in a society that is devoid of plot. And in an affective society, it is impossible to act. It might be possible to derive polygamy, or the 'polyamorous' society – an awful expression – from the capitalist or neoliberal mode of production. Maximize your options – and maximize the possibility of affect. The economic mode of production is also reflected in the dimension of love.

FB: In *The Agony of Eros* you say that the other is disappearing. What do you mean by that?

BCH: We have abolished the other, his negativity, in the name of freedom. In the name of freedom, we have also eliminated anything suggestive of a master, like God or the phallus. There's a story of a Japanese artist who cut off his phallus, ordered a head chef to cook it and then invited people, via Twitter, to eat his penis. He turned it into a performance. His guests ate the phallus. He wanted to be free, independent of sex. He wanted to be able to take on any identity. There is a price to pay for this total freedom: a lack of orientation, a lack of commitment. We have no one opposite us, no other. We just face ourselves.

TO: You mention the problem of faithfulness. Why do you think it is that so many people in our society have a problem with faithfulness?

BCH: Faithfulness and productivity are mutually exclusive. It is unfaithfulness that furthers growth and productivity. But I would like to return to our topic. In your eyes, the theatre of the future is a place free from economic compulsion. I also have a vision of the theatre of the future. It should be a theatre of silence. Maybe we have the same thing in mind. Capitalism dislikes silence.

COVID-19 Has Reduced Us to a 'Society of Survival'

A Conversation with Carmen Sigüenza and Esther Rebollo of EFE, the Spanish International News Agency

EFE: COVID-19 has democratized human vulnerability. Do you think we are now more fragile and more easily manipulated? Will we fall more easily into the hands of authoritarianism and populism?

Byung-Chul Han: COVID-19 is currently showing that human vulnerability or mortality is not democratic but depends on social status. Death is not democratic. COVID-19 hasn't changed anything either. Death has never been democratic. The pandemic in particular reveals social upheaval and differences in respective societies. Think about the United States. African-Americans are dying in disproportionate numbers from COVID-19 compared to other groups. The situation is similar in France. What good is the curfew if the suburban trains connecting Paris with lower income suburbs are jam-packed. The working poor with an immigrant background from urban banlieues contract and die of COVID-19. You have to work.

Home office workers cannot afford caregivers, factory workers, cleaners, sellers or garbage collectors. The rich, on the other hand, retreat to their country villa. The pandemic is therefore not only a medical problem, but also a social one. Another reason why not that many people have died in Germany is that social problems are not as serious there as in other European countries and the US. The healthcare system in Germany is also much better than in the US, France, England or Italy. But even in Germany, COVID-19 exposes social differences. In Germany, too, the socially weak die earlier. Poor people who cannot afford a car are crowding into full buses, trams and metros. COVID-19 shows that we live in a society of two classes. The second problem is that COVID-19 is not conducive to democracy. As is widely known, fear is the cradle for autocracy. In a crisis, people long for strong leaders again. Viktor Orbán is benefitting massively from it. It establishes the state of emergency as normal. And that is the end of democracy.

EFE: Freedom or security. What is the price we will pay to fight the pandemic?

BCH: In the face of the pandemic, we are heading for a biopolitical surveillance regime. Not only in our communication but also our bodies: our health will be subject to digital surveillance. According to Canadian author Naomi Klein, the crisis is a moment that heralds a new system of rules. The pandemic shock will ensure that a digital biopolitics takes hold globally that, with its control and monitoring system, seizes control of our bodies in a biopolitical disciplinary society that also constantly monitors our state of health. Faced with the shock of the pandemic, the West will be forced to give up its liberal principles. Then the West faces a biopolitical quarantine society that permanently restricts our freedom.

EFE: What are the consequences of fear and insecurity in people's lives?

BCH: The virus is a mirror. It shows what society we live in. We live in a survival society that is ultimately based on fear of death. Today survival is absolute, as if we were in a permanent state of war. All the forces of life are being used to prolong life. A society of survival loses all sense of the good life. Enjoyment is also sacrificed for health, which, in turn, is raised to an end in itself. The rigour of the no-smoking paradigm testifies to the hysteria of survival. The more life is one of survival, the more fear you have of death. The pandemic makes death, which we have carefully suppressed and outsourced, visible again. The constant presence of death in the mass media makes people nervous.

The hysteria of survival makes society so inhumane. Your neighbour is a potential virus carrier, someone to stay away from. Older people have to die alone in their nursing homes because nobody is allowed to visit them because of the risk of infection. Is prolonging life by a few months better than dying alone? In our hysteria of survival, we completely forget what a good life is. For survival, we willingly sacrifice everything that makes life worth living: sociability, community and proximity. In view of the pandemic, the radical restriction of fundamental rights is uncritically accepted.

Religious services are prohibited even at Easter. Priests also practise social distancing and wear protective masks. They totally sacrifice faith for survival. Charity manifests itself as keeping a distance. Virology disempowers theology. Everyone is listening to the virologists who have absolute sovereignty of interpretation. The narrative of resurrection completely gives way to the ideology of health and survival. In the face of the virus, belief degenerates into a farce. And our Pope Francis? Saint Francis hugged lepers . . . The fear and panic of the virus are exaggerated. The average age of those who died of COVID-19 in Germany is 80 or 81. The average life expectancy in Germany is 80.5. Our panicked reaction to the virus shows that something is wrong with our society.

EFE: Will our society after the coronavirus respect nature more and be more just and fair? Or does it make us more selfish and individualistic?

BCH: There is a fairy tale 'Sindbad the Seafarer'. On a trip, Sindbad arrives at a small island that looks like the garden of Eden. He and his companion feast and enjoy walks on the island. They light a fire and celebrate. Then the island suddenly bends. Trees bend. The island was actually the back of a giant fish that had been motionless for so long that a lot of sand had washed up and trees had grown on it. The heat of the fire on its back has upset the giant fish. It dives deep, and Sindbad is thrown into the sea. This fairy tale is a parable: it teaches that there is fundamental blindness in man. He is not even able to see what he is standing on, so he is working on his own downfall. In view of its rage to destroy, the German writer Arthur Schnitzler compares humanity to an illness. We act like bacteria or a virus on the earth, ruthlessly multiplying and ultimately destroying the host itself. Growth and destruction come together. Schnitzler believes that humans can only recognize primitive orders. Humans are just as blind to higher orders as the bacteria.

So the history of mankind is an eternal struggle against the divine, which is necessarily destroyed by the human. The pandemic is a result of human ruthlessness. We ruthlessly intervene in a sensitive ecosystem. Palaeontologist Andrew Knoll teaches that man is just the icing on the cake of evolution. The actual cake consists of bacteria and viruses that threaten to break through, or even recapture, that fragile surface at any time. Sindbad the sailor, who believes the back of a fish to be a safe island, is a permanent metaphor for human ignorance. Man thinks he is safe, while it is only a matter of time before he is thrown into the abyss by elemental forces. The violence he does to nature strikes back at him with greater force. This is the dialectic of the Anthropocene. In this age of man, man is more threatened than ever.

EFE: Is COVID-19 a mortal wound for globalization?

BCH: The principle of globalization is maximizing profits. For example, the manufacture of medical devices such as protective masks or medication has been moved to Asia. In Europe and the US, that has cost a lot of lives. Capital is misanthropic. We no longer do business for people, but for capital. Marx said that capital reduces man to its reproductive organ. Individual freedom, which today has become excessive, is ultimately nothing more than the excess of capital itself. We freely exploit ourselves in the belief that we are fulfilling ourselves. But in reality, we are servants. Kafka has pointed out the paradoxical logic of self-exploitation: the animal wrests the whip from the master and whips itself to become master. In such an absurd situation, people are in the neoliberal regime. Man has to regain freedom for himself.

EFE: Will the coronavirus and its consequences change the world order? Who will win the struggle for control and hegemony of world power? Will China step up against the US?

BCH: COVID-19 is probably not a good omen for Europe and the US. The virus is a physical test. Asian countries, which think little of liberalism, got a grip on the pandemic quite quickly, especially with their digital biopolitical surveillance, which is unimaginable for the West. Europe and the US are stumbling. In the face of the pandemic, they are losing their radiance. Žižek has claimed that the virus will bring down China's regime. Žižek is wrong. None of that will happen. The virus does not stop China's advance, quite the contrary. China will now also sell its autocratic surveillance state as a successful model against the epidemic. China will demonstrate the superiority of its system to the world with even more pride. COVID-19 will ensure that the world power moves a little further to Asia. Seen in this way, the virus marks the change of an era.

Edited by Zoran Radosavljevic

'I Am Sorry, But These Are the Facts'

A Conversation with Niels Boeing and Andreas Lebert

Byung-Chul Han has suggested that we meet at the Café Liebling at Prenzlauer Berg. The philosopher teaches at the Berlin University of the Arts, and he has caused a stir with his books on The Burnout Society *and* The Transparency Society. *Han, a shy man, generally avoids interviews.*

He is ten minutes late. Is he going to stand us up? No, here he comes, cycling down the street. He sits down and orders a cola.

Niels Boeing and Andreas Lebert: Where have you come from?

Byung-Chul Han: From my desk, as usual.

NB/AL: What are you working on?

BCH: I am writing a new book on beauty. I decided to embark on it after reading an interview with Botho Strauß. When asked 'What do you miss?' Botho Strauß replies: 'Beauty'. More he did not say. Just 'I miss beauty', and I understood what he meant. Then, I thought, 'I am going to write a book on beauty.'

NB/AL: You are thinking about beauty. What are you thinking, more specifically?

BCH: Thinking consists of the perception of similarities. I often have the experience that I suddenly perceive similarities between events, between a current event and an earlier one. Or between things that take place concurrently. I trace these relations.

NB/AL: And what does this mean in the case of beauty?

BCH: I perceive a connection between different things that are happening today, or are popular today. For example, Brazilian waxing, the sculptures of Jeff Koons, and the iPhone.

Niels Boeing and Andreas Lebert had expected that Byung-Chul Han's philosophical outlook would put them in a rather sombre mood. But after four hours of conversation, there was an almost buoyant atmosphere. Maybe this confirms Han's thesis that an excess of positivity causes depression?

NB/AL: You see similarities between the removal of body hair and a smartphone and an artist?

BCH: The commonality isn't that difficult to see: it is the smooth. Smoothness is a characteristic of our present. Do you know the *G Flex*, a smartphone by LG? This smartphone has a special covering. If it gets scratched, the scratch quickly disappears. That is, it has a self-healing skin, almost an organic skin. The smartphone therefore remains perfectly smooth. I ask myself: What is the problem with an object getting a few scratches? Why this striving for a smooth surface? And straightaway a connection opens up between the smooth smartphone, smooth skin, and love.

NB/AL: Love? That you need to explain.

BCH: The smooth surface of the smartphone is a skin that cannot be damaged, that can avoid any injury. And isn't it the case that today we seek to avoid any kind of harm in love as well? We do not want to be vulnerable; we shy away from hurting and from being hurt. Love requires a high level of commitment, but we avoid this commitment because it leads to us being hurt. Passion is avoided. Falling in love is already too painful.

Falling in love is no longer feasible. In French, one would say '*tomber amoureux*'. This kind of falling is too negative; it is already an injury to be avoided. This, for me, is linked up with another thought . . .

We live in the age of the 'Like'. Facebook does not have a 'Dislike' button, only a 'Like' one. And the 'Like' accelerates communication, while the 'Dislike' makes communication stutter. Injuries also make communication stutter. Even art seeks to avoid injury. There is no damage to be found on a Jeff Koons sculpture – no tears, no fault lines, no sharp edges, no seams either. Everything flows in soft and smooth transitions. It all appears rounded, polished, smoothed out – Jeff Koons's art is dedicated to the smooth surface. Today, a culture of agreeableness is emerging.[1] This is also true of politics.

NB/AL: A smooth politics is emerging?

BCH: Contemporary politics also shies away from strong commitments. This creates a politics of agreeableness. Who might the typical 'agreeable' politician be? Maybe Angela Merkel. That is what makes her so popular. She does not seem to have any firm convictions, any vision. She looks at the people on the street, and she bases her opinion on the mood on the street. After the nuclear disaster in Fukushima she was suddenly against nuclear power. One might say she is as slippery as an eel.[2] We are indeed dealing with a smooth politics.

There is an interesting connection between smooth skin, smooth art and smooth politics. But genuine political action requires vision and strong commitment. It must also be able to hurt. Today's smooth politics, however, does not do that. Not just Angela Merkel but all today's politicians are incapable of taking painful decisions. They are just the agreeable stooges of the system. When the system malfunctions, they do the repair work, and they do so while projecting the beautiful illusion that there is no alternative. Politics, however, has to offer alternatives. Otherwise there is nothing to distinguish it from dictatorship. We live in a dictatorship of neoliberalism. Within neoliberalism each of us is an entrepreneur of his own self. In Marx's time, capitalism had an altogether different labour structure. The economy consisted of factory owners and factory workers, and no factory worker was an entrepreneur of himself. What we had was exploitation by others. Today, we have self-exploitation – I exploit myself in the illusion that I actually find personal fulfilment.

NB/AL: This is why the notion of neoliberalism is often seen as a concept used by the left in political battle.

BCH: That is not correct. The term 'neoliberalism' captures well the condition of today's society as one that exploits freedom. The system wants to constantly increase productivity, and it switches from exploitation by others to self-exploitation because the latter is more efficient and more productive – and all this under the guise of freedom.

NB/AL: Your analysis doesn't sound very encouraging. We exploit ourselves. We do not take any risks, either in love or in politics. We do not want to get hurt and do not want to hurt others.

BCH: I am sorry, but these are the facts.

NB/AL: How can an individual find happiness in such a society? Should we do more to fight for our ideals?

BCH: The system makes this difficult. And we do not even know what we want. What I take to be my needs are not my real needs. Take the discount clothing shop Primark. People organize carpools to go there because there isn't a Primark near where they live. When they get there, they practically ransack the place. A newspaper article I came across the other day spoke about a girl who, upon learning that a Primark was to open next door to a C&A on Alexanderplatz, shrieked for joy, saying that when Primark arrived her life would be complete. Is this life really perfect for her, or is it an illusion created by this consumer culture? Let us take a close look at what is actually happening here. Girls buy a hundred items of clothing, each costing, say, five euros – that in itself is madness, because for clothes like this to exist people in countries like Bangladesh are dying when the textile factories they work in collapse. So the girls buy a hundred items of clothing, but they hardly ever wear them. Do you know what they do with them?

NB/AL: They present the clothes in haul videos on YouTube.

BCH: Exactly. They produce commercials with them! They create innumerable videos advertising the clothes they have bought, and they play at being models. Each of these YouTube videos is then viewed half a million times. Consumers buy clothes or other things but they do not use them; they produce commercials, and these commercials generate more consumption. That means an absolute form of consumption has emerged, a form which is de-coupled from the use of things. Businesses have delegated advertising to their consumers. They do not need to advertise themselves. That is a perfect system.

NB/AL: Should people protest against this?

BCH: Why should I protest against the arrival of Primark if that makes my life complete?

NB/AL: You write in your new book, *Psychopolitics*, that 'freedom will have been an episode'. Why?

BCH: Freedom is a counterpart of compulsion. If you experience the compulsion to which you are subjected, and of which you are not aware, as freedom, then that is the end of freedom. That is why we are in a crisis. The crisis of freedom consists in the fact that we perceive compulsion as freedom. In this situation, no resistance is possible. If you force me to do something, I can defend myself against this external compulsion. But if there is no longer an opponent who forces me to do something, then resistance is no longer possible. That is why the motto that opens my book is 'Protect me from what I want', a famous line from the artist Jenny Holzer.

NB/AL: Do we have to protect ourselves against ourselves, then?

BCH: When a system attacks freedom, I need to defend myself. The insidious aspect, however, is that now the system does not attack freedom but instrumentalizes it. Here is an example: when there was a census in the eighties, everyone took to the streets. A bomb was even planted in an administrative building. People demonstrated because they had an enemy, the state, that was seeking to wrest information from them against their will. Today, we disclose more data about ourselves than ever before. Why are there no protests? Because now, unlike in the eighties, we feel free. Back then, people felt that their freedom was under attack, that it was being diminished. And that is why they took to the streets. Today, we feel free. We voluntarily hand over our data.

NB/AL: Maybe because the smartphone can help us get to where we want to go. We consider the advantages to outweigh the disadvantages.

BCH: Possibly, but structurally this society does not differ from the feudalism of the Middle Ages. We live in bondage. The feudal lords of the digital, like Facebook, give us some land and say: 'Cultivate it. You can have it for free.' And we cultivate it exhaustively, this land. At the end of it all, the feudal lords return for the harvest. That is an exploitation of communication. We communicate with each other, and we feel free when we do so. The feudal lords extract capital from this communication. And the secret services monitor them. This system is extremely efficient. There are no protests against it because we live in a system that exploits freedom.

NB/AL: How do you deal with this at a personal level?

BCH: Like all of us, I get nervous when I am not online, of course; I am also one of the victims. Without all this digital communication, I could not practise my profession, whether as a professor or as a writer of books and articles. Everyone is integrated, is part of it.

NB/AL: What role do Big Data technologies play?

BCH: An important one, because Big Data is not only used for surveillance but most of all for controlling human behaviour. And when human behaviour is controlled, when the decisions we make are totally manipulated, even while we feel we take them voluntarily, then our free will is threatened. This means that Big Data puts our free will in jeopardy.

NB/AL: You say that Big Data leads to a new, classless society.

BCH: Today's digital society is not a classless society. Take the Big Data company Acxiom. It categorizes people. The lowest category is called '*waste*' – rubbish. Acxiom trades the data of about 300 million US citizens – that is, almost all US citizens. This company now knows more about US citizens than does the FBI, probably also more than does the NSA. At Acxiom, people are divided into seventy categories; they are offered up in a catalogue like commodities, with a product for every possible need. Consumers with a high market value are to be found in a category named 'shooting stars': they are aged twenty-six to forty-five; are dynamic; get up early to go running; have no kids, though they may be married; practise a vegan lifestyle; like to travel; and watch *Seinfeld*. That is how Big Data leads to the emergence of a new class society.

NB/AL: And who makes up the class called 'waste'?

BCH: Those with low scores. They will not get approved for credit, for instance. And thus, next to the panopticon, Jeremy Bentham's ideal prison, we have a ban-opticon, as the sociologist Zygmunt Bauman has called it.[3] The panopticon controls the locked-up inmates of a system; the ban-opticon, by contrast, is a dispositif which identifies people who are hostile to the system as unwanted and excludes them. The classical panopticon serves the purpose of discipline; the ban-opticon, by contrast, ensures the security and efficiency of the system. Interestingly, the NSA and Acxiom, that is, the secret service and the market, collaborate with one another.

NB/AL: Could the 'waste' class reach critical mass at some point, such that the control society will no longer be able to deal with it?

BCH: No. The members hide themselves away. They are ashamed. They are, for instance, 'Hartzer'.[4] They are in a state of constant fear. The fear in which the Hartzer have to live here is insane. They are kept in this ban-opticon to make sure that they do not escape their cells of fear. I know many Hartzer; they are treated like rubbish. In one of the richest countries in the world, in Germany, people are treated like scum. They are deprived of their dignity. Of course, because they feel ashamed, these people do not protest. Instead of holding society responsible, they accuse themselves. You cannot expect this class of people to act politically.

NB/AL: That is pretty depressing. Where will all this end?

BCH: Well, it certainly cannot go on like this, if only because of material resources. The oil may last for another fifty years. Here in Germany, we live under an illusion. We have largely moved production elsewhere. Our computers, our clothes, our smartphones are produced in China. But the desert is coming closer and closer to Beijing, and one can hardly breathe there because of the smog. When I was in Korea, I saw these yellow clouds of dust even reaching Seoul. You had to wear a protective mask – the particulates damage the lungs. The developments there are dramatic. Even if it will still be fine for a while, what kind of life is this? Or look at the people who fit all sorts of sensors to their bodies, measure their blood pressure, blood sugar level and body fat around the clock, and then put the data on the internet! It's called self-tracking. These people are already zombies; they are puppets whose strings are pulled by unknown forces, as Georg Büchner says in *Danton's Death*.

It should be mentioned that at this point our conversation in Café Liebling was frequently in danger of being interrupted by street musicians who came to our table, with their instruments dangerously close to our recording device, and cheerfully struck up a tune. There was a saxophonist playing the hits of Glenn Miller, a Parisian-style accordion player, and a guitarist singing 'Que Sera, Sera'. But Byung-Chul Han spoke with great concentration. It felt as though you could see him in the process of forming his thoughts until, at last, they became sentences, which he then strung together with precision. At these moments, his attention was fully focused on his thoughts – and not on the people to whom he was presenting them. The musical entertainment could not distract him.

NB/AL: Professor Han, you initially studied metallurgy in South Korea. What happened to turn the prospective engineer of metal technology Byung-Chul Han into the philosopher and relentless critic of the system?

BCH: I am a technophile. As a child, I enjoyed tinkering around with radios and other electronic and mechanical devices. I actually wanted to study electrical or mechanical engineering, but I ended up with metallurgy. I really was an enthusiastic engineer and tinkerer.

NB/AL: And why did you stop?

BCH: Because, on one occasion, when experimenting with chemicals, there was an explosion. I still have the scars today. I almost died, or I was at least almost blinded.

NB/AL: Where did that happen?

BCH: At my home in Seoul. I was a schoolboy. I spent the whole day tinkering, milling, soldering. My drawers were filled with wires, measuring devices and chemicals. I was a kind of alchemist. Metallurgy, after all, is a modern-day kind of alchemy. But after the explosion I stopped. I still tinker today, but not with wires or soldering irons. Thinking is also tinkering, and thinking can produce explosions. Thinking is the most dangerous activity, maybe more dangerous than the atomic bomb. It can change the world. That is why Lenin said: 'Learn, learn and learn!'

NB/AL: Do you want to hurt people?

BCH: No. I try to describe what is there. It is difficult to see through things. That is why I try to see more – to learn to see. I write down what I have seen. It might be, after all, that my books hurt because I describe things that one does not want to see. It is not me, not my analysis, that is merciless, but the world in which we live that is merciless, mad and absurd.

NB/AL: Are you a happy person?

BCH: That is not a question I ask.

NB/AL: Do you mean that is not a question one should ask?

BCH: It is really a meaningless question. Also, happiness is not a condition I want to achieve. You need to define the concept. What do you mean by 'happiness'?

NB/AL: That's simple: I like to be alive. I feel at home in the world, enjoy the world, sleep well.

BCH: Let's begin with the last point. I sleep poorly. The day before yesterday, I opened a symposium with the philosopher Wilhelm Schmidt, whose topic was the good life, with some music: the *Goldberg Variations*. Bach composed the *Goldberg Variations* for a count who suffered from severe insomnia. I reminded the audience of the first sentence of Marcel Proust's *In Search of Lost Time*. In the German version it says: 'Lange Zeit bin ich früh schlafen gegangen.' ['For a long time I used to go to bed early.'] But in French it says: 'Longtemps je me suis couché de bonne heure.' Bonheur means happiness. Thus, the correct translation would be: 'For a long time I went to bed happy.' I told the audience that being able to sleep well is a sign that one is leading a good, happy life. I myself suffer from sleep problems.

NB/AL: What do you do when you are unable to sleep?

BCH: What do I do? I lie there. On the other point: do I like to be alive? How can you like to exist in this false world? That is impossible. That is also why I am not happy. I rarely understand the world. It appears quite absurd to me. You cannot be happy living in absurdity. To be happy takes a lot of illusions, I think.

NB/AL: You enjoy . . .?

135

BCH: Enjoy what?

NB/AL: Anything!

BCH: The world I cannot enjoy.

NB/AL: A nice piece of cake?

BCH: I don't eat cake. I could enjoy a nice meal, but the food in Berlin, in Germany, is a problem. The Germans do not seem to appreciate good food. Maybe that is the fault of Protestantism, this aversion to the sensual. In Asia, an altogether different value is attached to food, a very great one. A lot of money is spent on it as well, unlike in Germany. Japan, for instance: there, eating is a cult and has an aesthetic. The incredible freshness of everything! Even nice-smelling rice would be enough to make you happy.

NB/AL: That sounds like a tiny bit of happiness after all. You have lived in Germany for thirty years. How did you endure that?

BCH: I would not say 'endure'. I like living in Germany. I love the quietness here. In Seoul I don't have that. Most of all I love the German language, its words. You can sense that when reading my books. Here I have a language in which I can philosophize very well. Yes, there are things I enjoy here – not so much the food, but Bach, played by Glenn Gould. I often listen to Bach for hours. I am not sure whether I would have stayed in Germany so long without Bach, without Schubert's *Winter Journey*, without Schumann's *Poet's Love*. Besides studying philosophy, I used to sing a lot, especially songs by Schumann and Schubert, and I also took a lot of singing lessons for it. To sing *Winter Journey*, accompanied by a piano, that is very beautiful . . .

NB/AL: So, there is beauty after all! You spend a lot of time talking the world down.

BCH: Maybe. Indeed, I make my students despair because I tell them about all these problems in my lectures. When I said at the meeting before the last, 'Today, we shall try to think of some solutions', there was applause. 'Finally! He is now going to deliver us from our despair.'

NB/AL: Excellent. Solutions are a topic we also wanted to talk with you about.

BCH: I wanted to work towards some solutions, but I only described further problems.

NB/AL: Okay, then, what are the further problems?

BCH: There is no language today – there is a speechlessness and a cluelessness. Today, language is being deprived of language. On the one hand, there is an enormous noise, communicative noise, on the other, an enormous muteness. And this muteness differs from silence. Silence is eloquent. But noise and muteness lack language. There is nothing but speechless, noisy communication. That is a problem. Today, there is not even knowledge, only information. Knowledge is something altogether different from information. The terms 'knowledge' and 'truth' sound very outdated. Knowledge also has an altogether different temporal structure. It stretches between the past and the future, while the temporality of information is the now, the present tense. Knowledge rests on experience. A master has knowledge at his disposal. Today, we live under the terror of dilettantism.

NB/AL: What do you call what the sciences do? Do they not create knowledge?

BCH: Today's scientists do not reflect on the social context of knowledge. They practise positive research. All knowledge is situated within relations of domination. A new relation of domination, a new dispositif, generates a new kind of knowledge, a new discourse. Knowledge is always embedded in a structure of domination. It is possible simply to practise positive research without recognizing that one is under the spell of this power, and without becoming aware of the contextual aspect of knowledge. There is no reflection on contextuality today. Philosophy is also becoming a positive discipline. It does not relate to society but only to itself. It thus becomes socially blind.

NB/AL: Do you think this is true of all academic activities?

BCH: More or less. What we have is a Google science that does not critically reflect on its own activities. The humanities need to think critically about their own activities, but they do not do this. Many people, for instance, research the emotions. Sometime I would like to ask someone involved in this research: why do you do what you do? They do not think about their own work.

NB/AL: What is your suggestion?

BCH: What is the social relevance of the humanities? That, in the end, is the question. You need to be clear about the social background of your own research, because all knowledge is embedded in the structure of domination that characterizes the system. Why are emotions being researched with such intensity today? Perhaps it is because emotions are now a factor of production. Emotions are used as means of control. If you can influence emotions, you can control and manipulate human behaviour on an unconscious level.

NB/AL: Now you sound like a conspiracy theorist. Would it be possible to create a better system by being more intelligent about it?

BCH: Intelligence is intel-legere, a reading in between, a distinction. Intelligence is the activity of drawing distinctions within a system. Intelligence cannot develop a new system, a new language. The mind is something altogether different from intelligence. I do not believe that a highly intelligent computer could copy the human mind. It is possible to design a highly intelligent machine, but the machine will never invent a new language, something altogether different – that I do not believe. A machine does not have a mind. No machine can bring forth more than it has taken in. That is exactly the essence of the miracle of life: that it can bring forth more than it has taken in, and that it brings forth something very different from what it has taken in. That is what life is. Life is mind. In that, it differs from the machine. But when it becomes mechanical, when everything comes to be dominated by algorithms, this life comes under threat. The immortal, mechanical human being imagined by post-humanists like Ray Kurzweil will no longer be a human being. Maybe one day it will be possible, with the help of technology, to achieve immortality, but we shall lose life in return. We shall achieve immortality at the price of life.

NOTES

Capitalism and the Death Drive

1 Walter Benjamin, 'The Work of Art in the Age of Its Technological Reproducibility' (Second Version), in *The Work of Art in the Age of Its Technological Reproducibility and Other Writings on Media*, Cambridge, MA: Harvard University Press, 2008, pp. 19–55; here p. 42.

2 Arthur Schnitzler, *Aphorismen und Betrachtungen*, Frankfurt am Main: S. Fischer, 1967, pp. 177f.

3 Sigmund Freud, *Civilization and Its Discontents*, New York: W. W. Norton, 1962 [1930], pp. 58f.

4 Transl. note: following James Strachey's translation of Freud's works, and according to Laplanche and Pontalis's *The Language of Psychoanalysis*, the English term for 'Todestrieb' is 'death instinct'. Here, I shall use the term 'death drive'. There are two reasons for this: it is by now more common in general academic usage, and it allows retaining the difference between 'Instinkt' (instinct) and 'Trieb' (drive).

5 Gilles Dostaler and Bernard Maris, *Capitalisme et pulsion de*

mort, Paris: Albin Michel, 2010, p. 9. ['La grande ruse du capitalisme, nous le verrons, est de canaliser, de détourner les forces d'anéantissement, la pulsion de mort vers la croissance.']

6 Sigmund Freud, *Beyond the Pleasure Principle*, New York: W. W. Norton, 1990 [1920], p. 46.

7 Ibid., p. 47 (transl. modified).

8 Ibid.

9 Freud, *Civilization and Its Discontents*, p. 66.

10 Ibid.

11 Ibid., p. 68.

12 Freud, *Beyond the Pleasure Principle*, p. 47.

13 Cf. Luigi De Marchi, *Der Urschock: Unsere Psyche, die Kultur und der Tod*, Darmstadt: Luchterhand, 1988.

14 Georg Baudler, *Ursünde Gewalt: Das Ringen um Gewaltfreiheit*, Düsseldorf: Patmos, 2001, p. 116.

15 E. S. Craighill Handy, *Polynesian Religion*, Honolulu: Bernice P. Bishop Museum Bulletin 34, 1927, p. 31; quoted after Elias Canetti, *Crowds and Power*, New York: Continuum, 1962, p. 251.

16 Adalbert von Chamisso, *The Wonderful History of Peter Schlemihl*, London: Peter Hardwicke, 1861 (transl. amended), at http://www.gutenberg.org/files/21943/21943-h/21943-h. htm (accessed 26 March 2020).

17 Jean Baudrillard, *Symbolic Exchange and Death*, Los Angeles: Sage, 1993, p. 127.

18 Transl. note: 'denn er bringt das Leben ums Leben'. 'Ums Leben bringen' is an expression that also means 'to kill'.

19 Erich Fromm, *The Anatomy of Human Destructiveness*, New York: Holt, Rinehart and Winston, 1973, p. 350.

20 Baudrillard, *Symbolic Exchange and Death*, p. 177 (transl. amended).

21 Ibid., p. 37 (transl. modified).

22 Norman O. Brown, *Life Against Death: The Psychoanalytical Meaning of History*, Middletown, CT: Wesleyan University Press, 1959, p. 284.

23 Georges Bataille, *Eroticism: Death and Sensuality*, San Francisco: City Lights Books, 1986 [1957], p. 239.

24 Ibid., p. 11.

25 Baudrillard, *Symbolic Exchange and Death*, p. 156.

26 Theodor W. Adorno, *Philosophische Terminologie*, Frankfurt am Main: Suhrkamp, 1974, vol. 2, pp. 181f.

27 Theodor W. Adorno, *Minima Moralia: Reflections from Damaged Life*, London: Verso, 2005 [1951], pp. 77f.

28 Sigmund Freud, 'Thoughts for the Times on War and Death', *Standard Edition*, Vol. XIV, London: Hogarth Press and the Institute of Psycho-analysis, 1957 [1915], pp. 273–302; here p. 299.

Why Revolution Is Impossible Today

1 Jeremy Rifkin, *The Zero Marginal Cost Society: The Internet of Things, the Collaborative Commons, and the Eclipse of Capitalism*, London: Palgrave Macmillan, 2014.

2 Transl. note: see e.g. Didier Bigo, 'Globalized (in)Security: the Field and the Ban-opticon', in Didier Bigo and Anastassia Tsoukala (eds), *Terror, Insecurity and Liberty: Illiberal Practices of Liberal Regimes After 9/11*, London: Routledge, 2008, pp. 10–48.

The Total Exploitation of the Human Being

1 Transl. note: see Carl Schmitt, *Political Theology: Four Chapters on the Concept of Sovereignty*, Cambridge, MA: MIT Press, 1985 [1922], p. 5.

2 Transl. note: quoted after Christian Linder, 'Freund oder Feind', *Lettre International* 68, 2005, p. 95.

3 Transl. note: Schufa, founded in 1927, originally stood for Schutzgemeinschaft für allgemeine Kreditsicherung [Protective association for general credit security]. Today, it has become the Schufa Holding AG, a private company based in Wiesbaden.

4 Transl. note: Martin Schulz was President of the European Parliament from 2012 to 2017.

5 Georg Büchner, *Danton's Death* (Act II, Scene 5), in *The Major Works*, New York: W. W. Norton, 2012, p. 52.

Inside the Digital Panopticon

1 Transl. note: see https://www.youtube.com/watch?v=zIE-5hg7FoA (last accessed 4 April 2020).
2 Transl. note: see https://marketing.acxiom.com/US-Parent-ReimaginingRetail-eb-Main.html?&utm_source=website&utm_medium=owned&utm_campaign=reimaginingretail (last accessed 4 April 2020).

Only What Is Dead Is Transparent

1 Ulrich Schacht, *Über Schnee und Geschichte: Notate 1983–2011*, Berlin: Matthes & Seitz, 2012 (diary entry for 23 June 2011).
2 Transl. note: 'parieren' means to obey without protest. It is often used of well-trained animals, or of people in whom very strict principles of education or military training have been inculcated.
3 Transl. note: Christian Wulff was President of the Federal Republic of Germany from 2010 to 2012. In 2012, he resigned over allegations of corruption, of which he was later acquitted, relating to his time as Minister President of Lower Saxony. In an interview in early 2012, he said he wanted to set a new standard of transparency and answer all the questions put to him.
4 Transl. note: see https://wiki.piratenpartei.de/Liquid_Democracy (last accessed 7 April 2020).
5 Georg Simmel, 'Marriage', in *The Sociology of Georg Simmel*, Glencoe, ILL: The Free Press, 1950, pp. 326–39; here p. 329 (transl. amended).
6 Peter Handke, *Am Felsfenster morgens (und andere Ortszeiten 1982–1987)*, Salzburg: Residenzverlag, 1998, p. 336.
7 Transl. note: see 'Die Welt retten', https://philomag.de/die-welt-retten (last accessed 8 April 2020) and 'Julian Assange

talks', https://www.asiasentinel.com/p/julian-assange-talks (last accessed 8 April 2020).

8 Transl. note: see Ilja Trojanow and Juli Zeh, *Angriff auf die Freiheit: Sicherheitswahn, Überwachungsstaat und der Abbau bürgerlicher Rechte*, Munich: Carl Hanser, 2009.

Torturous Emptiness

1 Transl. note: 'gratification crisis' refers to the imbalance between effort and reward at work according to the 'effort-reward-model' developed by the Swiss sociologist of medicine Johannes Siegrist. Rewards can be monetary or may come in the form of increased esteem or raised status.

2 Transl. note: 'Gegenstand' simply means object. By hyphenating the word, an additional meaning is created. 'Stand' can mean a position or stance. 'Gegen' means against. The compound thus expresses a stance, or object, that provides resistance.

Jumping Humans

1 Benjamin, 'The Work of Art in the Age of Its Technological Reproducibility', p. 27.

2 Transl. note: 'sich produzieren' has a double meaning: 'to produce oneself' and 'to show off' or 'perform'. The reflexive form is normally used with the second of these meanings.

3 Transl. note: 'face' here and where italicized in the remainder of the paragraph is in English in the original. 'Face' is most naturally translated as 'Gesicht'. 'Antlitz' (here translated as 'countenance') is a poetic expression for the face that is not, or at least is very rarely, used in everyday language. On the basis of its etymology, 'Antlitz' could be translated as 'that which looks out at you': an 'Antlitz' is a face with a gaze directed at you.

4 Friedrich Nietzsche, *Nachgelassene Fragmente: Herbst 1884 bis Herbst 1885*, Kritische Gesamtausgabe VII 3, Berlin: De Gruyter, 1974, p. 119.

5 Friedrich Nietsche, 'On the Uses and Disadvantages of History for Life', in *Untimely Meditations*, Cambridge: Cambridge University Press, 1997, pp. 57–123; here p. 60.

Where Do the Refugees Come From?

1 Jean Ziegler, *Betting on Famine: Why the World Still Goes Hungry*, New York: The New Press, 2013.
2 Transl. note: the Expo in Milan ran from May to October 2015, with the theme 'Feeding the Planet, Energy for Life'. Three of the seven sub-themes were 'Science for food safety, security and quality', 'Innovation in the agro-food supply chain', 'Technology for agriculture and biodiversity'.
3 Transl. note: International Human Rights and Conflict Resolution Clinic at Stanford Law School and Global Justice Clinic at NYU School of Law, *Living under Drones: Death, Injury, and Trauma to Civilians from the Use of Drone Practices in Pakistan*, 2012. The report is available at https://www-cdn. law.stanford.edu/wp-content/uploads/2015/07/Stanford-NYU-Living-Under-Drones.pdf (last accessed 2 December 2020).

Where the Wild Things Are

1 Immanuel Kant, 'Perpetual Peace: A Philosophical Sketch', in *Political Writings*, Cambridge: Cambridge University Press, 1970, pp. 93–130; here p. 104.
2 Ibid., p. 102.
3 Ibid., p. 103.
4 Ibid., p. 114.
5 Ibid., p. 106.
6 Ibid.
7 Ibid., p. 107 (transl. amended).
8 Ibid., p. 103 (transl. amended). Transl. note: the English translation softens the phrase 'European savages' somewhat, rendering it as 'savage nations of Europe'. However, Kant's term is 'europäische Wilde'. In fact, if anything, he judges

Europeans to be worse than cannibals: instead of eating their enemies, 'the Europeans know how to make better use of those they have defeated than merely by making a meal of them. They would rather use them to increase the number of their own subjects, thereby augmenting their stock of instruments for conducting even more extensive wars' (ibid.).

9 Ibid., p. 105.

10 Ibid., p. 108.

11 Ibid., p. 114.

12 Transl. note: 'Wer nur Mitleid empfindet, der hat keinen Verstand' – the title of a newspaper article by Henryk M. Broder in *Die Welt*, 25 August 2015, at https://www.welt.de/debatte/henryk-m-broder/article145576852/Wer-nur-Mitleid-empfindet-der-hat-keinen-Verstand.html (last accessed 3 December 2020).

13 Transl. note: see Immanuel Kant, *Groundwork for the Metaphysics of Morals*, New Haven: Yale University Press, 2002, p. 52: 'In the realm of ends everything has either a **price** or a **dignity**. What has a price is such that something else can also be put in its place as its *equivalent*; by contrast, that which is elevated above all price, and admits of no equivalent, has a dignity.'

14 Kant, 'Perpetual Peace', p. 103.

15 Ibid., p. 116.

16 Ibid., p. 125.

17 Ibid., p. 116.

Who Is a Refugee?

1 Hannah Arendt, 'We Refugees', in *The Jewish Writings*, New York: Schocken Books, 2007, pp. 264–74; here p. 264.

2 Ibid., p. 265.

3 Ibid.

4 Ibid., p. 272.

5 Ibid., p. 273.

6 Ibid., p. 272.

7 Transl. note: Frauke Petry, born 1975, was a leading politician of the far-right Alternative für Deutschland (Alternative for Germany). She left the party in September 2017, and is now an independent member of the Bundestag. She has announced that she will retire from politics when her term comes to an end in 2021. Alexander Gauland, born 1941, is a co-founder of the AfD and was co-leader from 2017 to 2019. He has been a member of the Bundestag since 2017. Björn Höcke, born 1972, is a member of the AfD's 'Der Flügel' (The Wing) group which has been declared a right-wing extremist organization by the German Federal Office for the Protection of the Constitution. He infamously called the Holocaust memorial in Berlin a 'memorial of shame'. A subsequent attempt by leading figures of the party to have him expelled failed in 2018. He is a member of the parliament of the federal state of Thuringia.

8 Transl. note: on 19 December 2016, Amri, born in Tunisia, carried out a terrorist attack at a Christmas market in Berlin, driving a lorry into the crowd and killing twelve people, including the lorry driver, whom Amri shot. A further fifty-five people were injured. Amri was shot and killed by Italian police in Sesto San Giovanni four days later. He had links with radical Islamist circles in Germany.

Beauty Lies Yonder, in the Foreign

1 Transl. note: the German is 'im Fremden', and the text uses 'fremd', 'Fremde', etc., throughout. While 'alien' or 'strange' would be the more natural choice in some instances, the translation consistently uses 'foreign' to maintain the unity of the phenomenon of 'das Fremde'.

2 Transl. note: an allusion to the Alternative für Deutschland, a far-right party that currently has eighty-nine seats in the Bundestag (as of July 2020).

3 Transl. note: two Korean dishes.

4 Theodor W. Adorno, 'On the Question: "What is German?"',

in *Critical Models: Interventions and Catchwords*, New York: Columbia University Press, 1998, pp. 205–14; here p. 214.

The Big Rush

1 Friedrich Nietzsche, *Human, All Too Human: A Book for Free Spirits*, Cambridge: Cambridge University Press, 1996, p. 133 (transl. modified).
2 Transl. note: on this, see Han, *The Scent of Time*, Cambridge: Polity, 2017, Chapters 1 and 2, esp. p. 5 and pp. 18f. 'Halt' can mean both 'stop' and 'support'. A 'Halterung' is a mount or bracket.
3 Transl. note: 'the tearing away of time' translates 'Fortriss der Zeit'. On the term 'Fortriss' and its Heideggerian context, see Han, *Scent of Time*, note 18 to Chapter 1, p. 117.
4 Transl. note: see Martin Heidegger, 'The Origin of the Work of Art (1935–36)', in *Off the Beaten Track*, Cambridge: Cambridge University Press, 2002, pp. 1–56; here p. 14.

In Your Face

1 'Am Rande. Wo sonst' [At the margins. Where else?], a conversation with Botho Strauß in *Die Zeit*, 14 September 2007.
2 Transl. note: 'facial' here and below in English in the original.
3 Transl. note: 'In your face' in English in the original.
4 Roland Barthes, *Mythologies*, London: Vintage, 1993, p. 90.
5 Jean Baudrillard, *Das Andere selbst*, Vienna: Edition Passagen, 1994, p. 27.
6 Walter Benjamin, 'Goethe's Elective Affinities', in *Selected Writings*, vol. 1 (1913–1926), Cambridge, MA: Harvard University Press, 1996, pp. 297–360; here p. 351.
7 Ibid., p. 352.
8 Johann Wolfgang Goethe, *Faust: Part II*, transl. David Constantine, London: Penguin, 2005, pp. 182f. (lines 9945–50). Transl. note: David Constantine's translation has here been substituted for the one used in Benjamin's *Selected Writings*.

9 Saint Augustine, *On Christian Doctrine*, no place: CreateSpace, 2015, p. 238.

10 Roland Barthes, *The Pleasure of the Text*, New York: Hill and Wang, 1975, p. 10.

11 Roland Barthes, *Camera Lucida*, New York: Farrar, Strauss & Giroux, 1999, p. 41.

12 Ibid., pp. 41f.

It Is Eros That Defeats Depression

1 Transl. note: an allusion to a *Spiegel* interview of 1966 with Martin Heidegger, published on 31 May 1976. As requested by Heidegger, it only appeared after his death. (Heidegger died on 26 May 1976.) Asked whether the individual or philosophy could do anything to influence the web of necessities that characterizes contemporary society, Heidegger replied: 'Only a god can still save us.' ('Nur noch ein Gott kann uns retten.') The interview can be found at http://la.utexas.edu/users/hcl eaver/330T/350kPEEHeideggerSpiegel.pdf, and in Richard Wolin (ed.), *The Heidegger Controversy*, Cambridge, MA: MIT Press, 1993, pp. 91–116. The original *Spiegel* interview at: https://bublitz.org/wp-content/uploads/2018/03/Heidegger-Spiegel-31–05–1976.pdf (last accessed 3 December 2020).

Capitalism Dislikes Silence

1 Transl. note: 'Schulden' are 'debts'. 'Schuld' means 'guilt'. Both meanings are invoked here in 'Entschuldung'.

2 Transl. note: 'Vermögen' means both 'wealth' and 'capacity'.

3 Transl. note: 'Wutbürger', referring to a group of mostly middle-class, politically disaffected citizens, was the 'word of the year 2010' in Germany.

4 'Noch nie einen Menschen von innen gesehen?' [Never seen a human being from the inside?], in *Frankfurter Allgemeine Zeitung*, 17 May 2010.

5 Byung-Chul Han, *The Agony of Eros*, Cambridge, MA: MIT Press, 2017, p. 13.

6   Transl. note: in German, 'Schaumbad' (bubble bath) is used in idiomatic expressions for overwhelming but at the same time superficial feelings: 'Emotionales Schaumbad' (emotional bubble bath) or 'Schaumbad der Gefühle' (bubble bath of feelings).

7   Transl. note: the letter actually begins: 'You're 82 years old. You've shrunk six centimetres, you only weigh 45 kilos yet you're still beautiful, gracious and desirable.' André Gorz, *Letter to D: A Love Story*, Cambridge: Polity, 2009, p. 1.

'I Am Sorry, But These Are the Facts'

1   Transl. note: 'Agreeableness' translates 'Gefälligkeit'. The German expression covers a range of meanings from something or someone being pleasant or agreeable, to doing someone a favour ('jemandem eine Gefälligkeit erweisen'). The core of all these meanings is the absence of tension or friction, of anything that might cause repulsion rather than attraction – in Han's terminology, the culture of smoothness refers to the absence of negativity and the rule of positivity.

2   Transl. note: the German for 'slippery as an eel' – 'aalglatt' – contains the word for 'smooth', 'glatt'.

3   Transl. note: the term 'ban-opticon' was in fact originally coined by Didier Bigo. See e.g. Bigo and Tsoukala (eds), *Terror, Insecurity and Liberty*.

4   Transl. note: 'Hartzer' refers to the recipients of benefits under 'Hartz IV', the German welfare benefit system.